GEORGE WASHINGTON

GEORGE WASHINGTON

ROBERT F. JONES

Revised Edition

New York
FORDHAM UNIVERSITY PRESS

Jones, Robert Francis, 1935-
    George Washington / by Robert F. Jones.

1. Washington, George, 1732-1799.
2. Presidents—United States—Biography.
I. Title.

E312 .J79 1996   973.4/1/0924

VXORI PVLCHRISSIMAE
ET SERENAE

Printed in the United States of America

Contents

Preface

John Adams was certainly not correct when he prophesied that the "History of our Revolution will be one continued lye from one end to the other" but he was considerably closer to the truth when he predicted that one of the more notable distortions of that history would be "that Dr. Franklin's electrified Rod smote the Earth and out sprung General Washington. . . . That Franklin electrified him with his rod—and thence forward these two conducted all the Policy, Negotiations, Legislatures and War." Properly, George Washington has figured large in the history of the achievement of American independence; yet, for all the ink spilt in his name, few Americans know more about him than a few stray facts and some stories, some true, some false, but all insignificant, about a cherry tree and a hatchet, dental problems, kneeling in prayer in the snows of Valley Forge and throwing a coin across a river. What I have done within these pages is to synthesize the best modern scholarship on Washington into a brief biography that will give the student or general reader an opportunity to gain a proper understanding of Washington's character and his contribution to the securing of American independence all the while setting the record straight on a few of the more notable "lyes" which John Adams predicted.

Any historian stands on the shoulders of those who have previously studied the problem, but most especially when writing a work of this sort. Although I have done some research in the Papers of George Washington at the Library of Congress, my primary reliance has been on the two most recent multi-volume biographies of Washington and other, more specialized, studies. Anyone wishing to compare this work with Douglas Southall Freeman's seven volumes (New York: Scribner's, 1948–57; completed by J.A. Carroll and M.W. Ashworth) or James Thomas Flexner's four volumes (Boston: Little, Brown, 1965–72) will recognize my debt to those gentlemen and I acknowledge it gratefully. If I had not been able to rely on the results of their labors, my own would have been considerably more arduous. But, perhaps perversely, I have not accepted their judgments in all cases, and what follows is not a condensation of previous work as much as my interpretation of it.

Many people have helped me in the preparation of this book; the staffs of the New-York Historical Society library, the New York Public Library, the Library of Congress manuscript division, and Duane Library of Fordham University were both competent and gracious in securing material for me. Fordham University awarded me a faculty fellowship, giving me sufficient free time to do the research necessary for this book. Jerome Bodian, M.D., helped me to understand and describe the nature of Washington's last illness; my Fordham colleagues John F. Roche and Joseph R. Frese, S.J., were always willing to let me pick their brains. Maria Eufemia, Ph.D., was my graduate assistant when I began my work on Washington and helped me compile the initial bibliography; selfishly, I wish I had had her competent help throughout my research and writing. William and Mary Henhoeffer generously accommodated me while I was working at the Library of Congress. My good friends Serge and Betty Hughes gave me one of the biggest advantages of all, a convenient, quiet place in which a writer with a large family and a small house could work. My daughter, Ann Leslie, has helped in tidying up the manuscript, putting pages in order, etc. The dedication is an attempt to say the unsayable. All these people have helped me to avoid errors, but they could not guarantee it; the discredit for any remaining is mine.

ROBERT F. JONES

Preface to the Revised Edition

I am gratified that the favorable reception given to my biography of George Washington has warranted the publishing of this revised edition. It not only is gratifying to my vanity, but will also put the work in a form more agreeable to my purpose in writing. I have also taken advantage of this opportunity to correct several errors in the text which slipped through in the first edition, as well as to supplement the Bibliography with some of the more recent work done on our first president. The reviews by Frederick H. Schmidt (*The Virginia Magazine of History and Biography* 88, No. 2 [April 1980]) and by Donald H. Stewart (*The Journal of American History* 67, No. 2 [September 1980]) have helped me in this work. Perhaps ungenerously, I have not followed them in all cases, sometimes insisting on my own reading of the material, but I appreciate their pertinent comments, especially Mr. Schmidt's.

On such an occasion, an author is often tempted to argue for extensive revisions in the text. Being of strong character, I have resisted this temptation, and I shall content myself here with treating two instances in which I now believe that I either omitted covering some pertinent material or misread the record. First, I believe that I admired Washington a bit too much for his switch to wheat cultivation (in place of tobacco) in the 1760s. It does not detract at all from his stature as an intelligent, systematic, and adaptable agriculturalist to note that there was a general turning-away from tobacco to wheat in the upper South at that time, a conversion with far-reaching economic and political effects, according to Joyce Appleby (in e.g., "Commercial Farming and the 'Agrarian Myth' in the Early Republic," *The Journal of American History* 68, No. 4 [March 1982], 833–49, esp. 839–40). Second, I believe that I was perhaps too generous in my estimate of Edmund Randolph, both in his service to President Washington and in my brief references to his character. Although I generally agree with the narrative as presented in John J. Reardon's *Edmund Randolph* (New York: Macmillan, 1974), I now lean toward Thomas Jefferson's characterization of him as a political "chameleon," a person with few fixed points of reference; perhaps also a person whom events contrived to lift above the level of his abilities. This should

9

not be taken, however, as a softening of my implicit criticism of Washington's conduct toward Randolph in the circumstances surrounding Randolph's resignation as Secretary of State in August 1795. Even a "chameleon" deserves his day in court.

Finally, I thank Fordham University Press for publishing *George Washington* in this convenient edition. My purpose in writing the book originally was to provide the student and general reader with a brief, readable, and reliable biography of Washington—a purpose well served, I am certain, by this new edition.

R. F. J.

Fordham University
November 1985

Chronology

1732 Feb. 22 (11 o.s.), born at Wakefield, Westmoreland Co., Virginia.

1743 April 12, death of father, Augustine W.

1753 Oct. 31–Jan. 16, 1754, delivery of Gov. Dinwiddie's ultimatum to the French.

1754 Mar.–Oct., first campaign against the French.

1755 Apr.–Jul., aide-de-camp to Gen. Braddock. Aug., appointment as Colonel of the Virginia Regiment.

1758 Jun.–Nov., Forbes expedition against Fort Duquesne. Jul. 24, elected burgess for Frederick Co. (served until Jul. 1765; elected for Fairfax Co., served until 1775). Dec., resignation of commission.

1759 Jan. 6, marriage to Martha Dandridge Custis.

1774 Sep.–Oct., Virginia delegate to First Continental Congress.

1775 May–Jun., Virginia delegate to Second Continental Congress. Jun. 16, elected General and Commander-in-Chief of the Army of the Continental Congress. Jul. 3, took command of the troops at Cambridge, Massachusetts.

1776 Mar. 17, occupied Boston. Aug. 26, Battle of Long Island. Oct. 28, Battle of White Plains. Dec. 25–Jan. 3, 1777, Trenton–Princeton Campaign.

1777 Sep. 11, Battle of Brandywine. Oct. 4, Battle of Germantown.

1778 Jun. 28, Battle of Monmouth.

1781 Aug.–Oct., Yorktown Campaign, ending in the surrender of Cornwallis, Oct. 19.

1783 Mar. 15, reply to "Newburgh Address" by mutinous officers. Dec. 23, resignation of commission before Congress at Annapolis, Maryland.

1787 May 25, elected president of the Constitutional Convention. Sept. 17, draft of Constitution signed and Convention adjourned.

1789 Feb. 4, unanimously elected President of the United States. Apr. 30, inaugurated at New York.

1790 Sept., took up residence in Philadelphia, temporary capital.

1792 Dec. 5, unanimously reelected President.

1793 Mar. 3, inaugurated president for second term at Philadelphia. Apr. 22, Neutrality Proclamation. Dec. 18, laid cornerstone of the Capitol at Washington, D.C.

1796 Sept. 19, publication of Farewell Address (dated Sept. 17) in Philadelphia *Daily American Advertiser*.

1797 Mar. 4, retirement following John Adams's inauguration.

1798 Jul. 4, appointment as Lieutenant-General and Commander-in-Chief of the Armies of the United States.

1799 Dec. 14, death at Mount Vernon (buried in family vault, Dec. 18).

CHAPTER 1

In the Service of Virginia, 1732–1758

If I can find it worthwhile pushing my fortune in the military way.

IT is a penetrating glimpse of the obvious to say that the event was not the least unusual, and there was no reason to suspect that anyone who noted it realized he was witnessing the start of a life which would help to revolutionize the English-speaking world: a Virginia planter and his second wife were blessed with their first child. On February 22, 1732, Mary Ball Washington gave birth to a baby boy who, some weeks later, was christened "George" after his mother's guardian. The birth took place at a plantation on Pope's Creek, one of several belonging to Augustine Washington, a third-generation Virginian. Since the 1650s, Washingtons had been active in Virginia affairs and had firmly established themselves in the middle rank of the colony's gentry. Augustine Washington did not rest content with what he inherited from his acquisitive ancestors, but enlarged his holdings, purchasing a tract on Little Hunting Creek, near the Potomac, in 1726, the nucleus of the future "Mount Vernon." He was astute enough to see that wealth lay not only with the land and invested in the Principio Iron Company, a venture mounted mainly by English Quakers.

The Virginia into which George had been born was a little more than a century old and still showed its youth; the frontier began within a day's ride of his birthplace. The West, the frontier, and the limitless challenge and opportunity which these words suggest were not abstractions but reality to the young man and much of his early life would be spent testing himself at the edge of settlement and beyond. But colonial Virginia was also the home of great plantations owned by an upper class who, as much as their circumstances permitted, lived in the style of the English gentry. A conspicuous difference, noted at once by anyone from old England, was the presence of black slaves as field hands and servants. Thus the Virginia of George's youth was a

13

land of sharp contrasts: cultivated fields and rough wilderness, polished gentry and ignorant bondsmen. It was an economy which, necessarily, lived off the land, cultivating the tobacco which had given it its first taste of prosperity and was still its most important product. But the price of tobacco had dropped to the point where it was only marginally profitable for many planters and the more enterprising had started to diversify their interests, as witness Augustine's investment in the Principio. The pattern of Virginia's trade, however, held most planters to tobacco. Trading directly with English or Scottish mercantile houses, they had incurred, or inherited, debts which had gradually converted them, in Thomas Jefferson's succinct phrase, into "a species of property annexed to certain English mercantile houses." Faced with large debts, most planters stayed with the one cash crop they knew, tobacco, while some of them looked to speculation in western lands for economic salvation, an unfulfilled hope for most of them. Virginia's tobacco economy had passed its peak and, in the future, prosperity would go to only the most enterprising and diligent planters.[1]

Young George, naturally, knew little of this as he played about the acres of the Little Hunting Creek plantation where the family had moved shortly after his birth. In 1739 Augustine gave the tract to a son of his first marriage, Lawrence, and moved the family—a sister and three brothers had followed George—to another plantation near Fredericksburg. After his father died in 1743, George divided his time between home and his half-brother, Augustine, Jr.'s, home on Pope's Creek. There, either from tutors or an infant school in the neighborhood, he learned to write in a clear hand and became, for someone who probably lacked the instinct of a good speller, reasonably adept in that arcane art. He also studied composition, geography, and deportment. Only in mathematics did his schooling go beyond the elementary level, and most of that seems to have been in the practical art of surveying. Little more than this can be said of his childhood, possibly the period most worked on by the mythmakers because there is so little evidence to go on.

His study of deportment was based on the *Rules of Civility and Decent Behaviour*, originally compiled by Jesuits as a guide to the children of the French aristocracy but, since its primary aim was to develop a consciousness of the effect one's behavior had on others, it could easily be used in the education of any youngster. Some of the more pertinent *Rules* (there were 110) were: #17, "Be no Flatterer . . .", #25, "Superfluous Compliments and all Affectations of Ceremonie are to be avoided, yet where due they are not to be Neglected", #82, "Undertake not what you cannot perform but be Carefull to keep your Promise."[2] No biographer can resist the temptation to trace out the adult character from such juvenile influences, but any such conclusions are obviously tentative. It is my opinion that the mature Washington generally kept to the letter and spirit of the *Rules* but the young adult in his ambition to get ahead violated several of them; once he had attained an assured position as a Virginia planter and, perhaps, a measure of self-confidence, his conduct toward others was almost always considerate and generous.

However incomplete his education and happy his childhood, the death of his father seriously affected George's present situation and future prospects. Although Augustine's estate was large, it had to be divided among seven children and his widow. George's share proved to be modest: "Ferry Farm," near Fredericksburg, 260 acres and ten slaves, one-half of the Deep Run tract (in all almost 2,200 acres in an area known for its poor soil), three town lots in Fredericksburg, and one-fifth of his father's residual personal property. All in all, not a splendid inheritance, it was just large enough to serve as a springboard for future advancement, but it was also just large enough to support George as a planter of modest fortune.

George's relationship with his mother is something of a puzzle; Mary Washington seems to have been a strong, domineering woman with an extraordinary amount of self-reliance. Freed by widowhood from immediate male direction, she henceforth sought advice from her brother, Joseph Ball, in London, far enough away to be safely ignored if necessary. George seems to have been uncomfortable with her and contrived to spend a good bit of time with his half-brothers, especially Lawrence. Mary's concern for her son was not entirely selfish; the famous incident where she refused to allow him to accept a proffered midshipman's post on a visiting Royal Navy vessel is a case in point. As Joseph Ball retroactively but correctly pointed out, young George lacked the "interest" needed to win advancement in the navy and fully approved of his sister's refusal. "Interest" was shorthand for the system of influence and preference by which English aristocrats pushed their chosen into positions of honor and profit; in England and throughout the Empire generally, merit had little, and who your friends were, much, to do with advancement under the Crown. Thus his career would almost certainly have been difficult and undistinguished. Whether or not George appreciated how correct his mother was on this occasion does not survive but he did submit to her decision. His attitude toward her combined, as one writer has suggested, distance and deference.[3] Throughout her long life—she died in 1789—he made certain she lacked nothing but visited her infrequently and never encouraged her to visit or live at Mount Vernon.

Although "interest" in England was beyond George, its Virginia equivalent was readily available. Lawrence, a kind of surrogate father, had married Anne Fairfax, the daughter of Colonel William Fairfax, agent and cousin of the Proprietor of the Fairfax Grant, initially practically all of northern Virginia. In 1747 the Proprietor himself, Thomas, Lord Fairfax chose to live on his lands and moved to a hunting lodge, Greenway Court, in the Shenandoah Valley. Thus through Lawrence, George was well connected with the Fairfaxes and became acquainted with a genuine English lord, albeit one who preferred foxhounds to ladies and the Shenandoah to Sussex.

More important than the lord in introducing Washington to the adult world were his brother Lawrence and Colonel Fairfax. Both had good educations and wide experience outside Virginia; when they spoke of their adventures, they may have set the boy to dreaming of similar glory. And both moved in a polished and glittering social circle, much different from the comfortable but crude circumstances of Ferry Farm or even Greenway Court. If George developed his inclination to a military career and his refined tastes from anything other than his own innate character, then a strong influence would be the society he took a youthful part in at "Mount Vernon," the name Lawrence gave the Hunting Creek acres, and the adjacent Fairfax plantation, "Belvoir."

His association with the Fairfaxes may have given him something far more valuable than an inclination to arms and a familiarity with gentle society. Samuel Eliot Morison has suggested that Colonel Fairfax acquainted George with Stoic philosophy, a philosophy of life which stressed the attainment of *virtus*, inadequately translated as virtue, a combination of wisdom, courage, self-control, and justice. In striving for this goal, one would put oneself beyond the touch of a rude and capricious fortune, would become as self-sufficient as possible. The end of this was not a removal from society, but rather a life of service and responsibility. As Seneca, the most useful of the Stoics, wrote: "plunge into the midst of public life . . . to try to gain office . . . attracted . . . by the desire to be more serviceable and useful to my friends and relatives and all my countrymen and then to all mankind." This commitment to public service, so prominent in his adult life, was reinforced for George by the example of those around him, all of whom were busy tending not only their own plantations, but also assisting in the political life of the colony. One may infer this same exemplification of the Stoic ideal from Marcus Cunliffe's comment that there was much in Washington's career and in the Virginia society of his youth that was Roman. Virtue was a goal, an end which would never be reached, but in the attempt to achieve it one could acquire two priceless gifts: an inner serenity and the well-merited applause of one's fellow citizens. It is difficult to think of a better model or set of precepts for someone whose life contained the trials and opportunities Washington's did.[4]

These were in the future, for now George certainly saw as more pressing the usual problems of adolescence. He was a big boy, somewhat gawky until he gained control of his body and blessed with a naturally strong constitution supplemented by the rude good health of youth. He seems to have had a natural aptitude for mathematics and somewhere learned the rudiments of surveying, not only useful for a landowner but also a skill much in demand in the constantly growing colony. He began to earn small sums running off simple assignments for neighbors before he was sixteen. He went along his friend George William Fairfax, the colonel's son, on a surveying party in the Shenandoah in 1748, where he got a firsthand taste of the frontier, which he and George William did not find especially to their liking as the two boys broke off and came home early. But he was careful to keep a detailed journal of the trip, soberly entering his judgment on some German squatters the party encountered—"as ignorant a set of people as the Indians," they could not even speak English! Despite the premature end to the trip, he had seen what the frontier required and, for a sixteen-year-old from comfortable circumstances, dealt satisfactorily with it.[5]

In 1749 George qualifed as the official surveyor for Culpeper County and could now sign surveys and work anywhere within the province. This gave him a modest but assured income, and within a year he had saved enough to buy almost 1,500 acres on Bullskin Creek in the Shenandoah. Late in 1751 he interrupted his surveying to accompany Lawrence, who had contracted tuberculosis, on a trip to Barbados. Not only did Lawrence not improve but George came down with smallpox and fought off the disease only with difficulty. He had returned to Virginia before the end of January 1752, thus ending the only trip he would ever make outside the continental limits of the future United States. He immediately resumed his surveying, and within two months was able to add another 500 acres to the Bullskin tract.

Despite his steady employment and land purchasing, he also had the usual concerns of any twenty-year-old and, in the spring of 1752, gave fair warning to William Fauntleroy that he would presently visit his plantation to secure "a revocation of the former cruel sentence" which Fauntleroy's fifteen-year-old daughter, Betsy, had imposed; like some of his later campaigns, this one also was a failure. This was not his first disappointment in romance; earlier he had been taken with an unnamed "lowland beauty," and sometime around 1748 had started an acrostic poem to Frances Alexander; although he managed to get past the X with "Xerxes that great, was't free from Cupid's dart," the poem was never finished. Probably, as in most such efforts, either Frances, or George, or Cupid, or possibly all three, lost interest.[6]

This busy, happy life was marred by Lawrence's death in July 1752, a loss which deprived George of the person to whom he had looked the most for guidance; he had lost more than a guardian and a brother; he had lost a friend. His regard for Lawrence was seen in his refusal to rename Mount Vernon when he rented it from Lawrence's widow, Ann Lee, in 1754. When she died, in 1761, the estate became his, according to the terms of Augustine's will. Another kind of bequest came in George's appointment as adjutant of the Northern Neck district, in charge of militia training, a post formerly held by Lawrence and carrying with it a provincial commission as a major and a salary of £100 a year. Coming, as it did, almost on his twenty-first birthday, Major Washington may have regarded his commission as a kind of birthday gift and reflected that, for a younger son of small fortune and uncertain prospects, he had not done badly since his father's death ten years before. He now had assured employment as a surveyor, owned almost 5,000 acres of land in various parcels, had good health, having already survived malaria, smallpox, and pleurisy, could travel and survive in the wild, and, for someone with limited formal education, write a reasonably good letter. He was well equipped to open a new act in his life; he would try, as he later put it, "to push his Fortune in the Military Way."

Washington's opportunity came because of a worldwide contest for empire and profit between England and France which had been going on since the end of the seventeenth century. Since 1748, there had been a truce in the struggle; although the truce could have been broken at any one of a dozen places around the globe, the break happened to come on the American frontier. In 1752–53 the French had begun to push south from Lake Erie, toward the Forks of the Ohio, present-day Pittsburgh, an area claimed by both Virginia and Pennsylvania. Robert Dinwiddie, Virginia's governor since 1751, regarded the American colonies as one of the richest assets of the Empire and did all he could to convince Virginia's penurious and unwilling legislature, the House of Burgesses, to head off French occupation of what was obviously the key to the Ohio Valley. Boosting his interest was a share in the Anglo-American Ohio Company, which had received a contingent land grant in the area. Into this tangle of imperial, colonial, and private selfishness with implications reaching far beyond even the vast area immediately concerned, Washington moved, hardly conscious of the consequences of his actions.

Governor Dinwiddie, an elderly Scot who was an energetic and reasonably effective administrator, had a charge from the king to secure the Forks against the French. The first step was to be a formal warning, and for this he needed a messenger. Possibly tipped off by Colonel Fairfax, Washington went to Williamsburg and secured the charge. He was directed to deliver the warning to the French commander and return with a reply and whatever knowledge of the strength and intentions of the French he could gather. Although the mission had its dangers, its successful fulfillment could bring the young man future preferment. By November 14, 1753, he had reached Wills Creek (later Cumberland, Maryland), where he convinced Christopher Gist, an experienced frontiersman, to accompany him. When he reached the Forks, he discovered the French were still in the north, but before he moved he gathered the friendly Indians for a conference. Here he showed his greenness in dealing with them. When the leader, Tanachariston, "the Half-King" (so called because his tribe, the Delaware, were vassals of the Iroquois), regaled him with a ferocious speech he had delivered to the French commander, instead of replying in kind, describing the immense power and implacable will of the English king, the major soberly asked the best way to French headquarters. But he learned fast and readily consented to wait while some ceremonial wampum belts, to be returned to the French as indicators of the Half-King's anger, were brought from another village. Fort LeBouef and the French commander were finally reached on December 11, and Washington delivered Dinwiddie's formal notice to the French that they were trespassing on the lands of the King of England. While waiting for the reply, the major readily determined that the French were going to

move south with the spring floods. He was also given some anxious
moments by French attempts to seduce the Indians, confiding to his
journal: "I can't say that ever in my Life I suffered so much Anxiety as
I did in this Affair." Despite the adolescent hyperbole, the comment
showed he appreciated the importance of the Indians to the success of
either side. He managed to get both the Indians and himself away on
December 16, and after an eventful and difficult trip—Washington
was shot at by an Indian whom he and Gist encountered, and he fell
into the icy Allegheny—he reached Wills Creek on January 2.
Leaving Gist, Washington rode alone to Williamsburg, delivering
the French reply, a polite but firm refusal to move until ordered by
their king, to Dinwiddie on January 16. Along with the reply,
Washington gave the governor valuable information on the strength
and intentions of the French and the solidity of the Indians' attachment to the English. All in all, a creditable performance by an
inexperienced twenty-one-year-old militia officer. To Washington's
surprise, Dinwiddie asked for a formal report and the major had to sit
up half the night throwing together a narrative from his rough notes.
Pleased with the report, the governor ordered it printed and
distributed throughout the colonies and copies sent to London, so
that, before he was twenty-two, Washington's name had spread well
beyond his own colony.[7]

Now that the aggressive intentions of the French in the area of the
Forks were known, Dinwiddie moved to place an English presence
there and bent all his efforts to convince the Burgesses to raise and
support a regiment of soldiers. After they had complied, the governor
added a land bounty of 200,000 acres on the Ohio to supplement the
enlisted mens' pay of eight pennies a day. Washington's interest was
not strong enough to secure him command of the force—that went to
Joshua Fry—but he was given the lieutenant colonelcy. Despite his
openly expressed disappointment of finding his salary much below
that of an officer on royal service, he accepted and, at Dinwiddie's
order, took the men already enlisted toward the Ohio; an independent command, at least until Colonel Fry caught up, was some
compensation. Although he was ordered to act defensively, he was
also to "restrain" any trespassers and "in Case of resistance to make
Prisoners of or kill and destroy them." If Dinwiddie wanted to put the
onus for starting any hostilities on the French, and such was the clear
intention of the Crown's orders to him, this was not made clear to his
subordinate.[8]

Arriving at Wills Creek with 159 ill-trained, ill-supplied men,

Washington learned that the French had pushed some men employed by the Ohio Company away from the Forks and begun a fort. He decided to push on toward the Forks, building a road as he went so that an attack could be more easily mounted once Fry arrived and also to reassure the Half-King, increasingly anxious about his alliance with the English. The hard work of road-building added to the discontent of Washington and, according to him, his officers over their inferior pay. News that two independent companies, whose officers were on royal service, were on their way, only increased the young officer's ire as those officers might also claim the superior authority their royal commissions, regardless of rank, gave them. This aroused all Washington's ire about his low pay and he angrily threatened Dinwiddie with his resignation if his pay was not raised to the royal standard; rather than dishonor himself by serving for a pittance, he would serve as an unpaid volunteer.

The force reached the Great Meadows, about fifty miles southeast of the Forks, in late May 1754, where Washington was told of a large French scouting party nearby. On the morning of May 28, the Virginians and some Indian allies surrounded the French and attacked them. In the brief skirmish that followed, several Frenchmen, including their commander, the Sieur de Jumonville, were killed. Only then did the French, who had been camped in a well-hidden glade, produce documents supporting their claim that their mission was peaceful, to deliver an order from their commander bidding the English to leave their lands. Washington rejected their claim; he reasoned that a peaceful party would not have hidden themselves away, nor were thirty men needed to deliver such a message. Implicitly he was using his own conduct the previous winter as a standard. Although the French claim was dubious, it sufficed to give them propaganda when later inadvertently reinforced by Washington.

In reporting to the governor, the young officer clearly showed what was most on his mind. Only after repeating most of his complaints about pay and conditions of service did he tell Dinwiddie about the skirmish and its results. He described the encounter more vividly to his brother, concluding with the self-confident observation: "I heard the bullets whistle, and, believe me, there is something charming in the sound." Realizing that the French were probably in force in the area, Washington pulled up short at the Meadows and began to build a small post, "Fort Necessity." Presently he learned of Fry's death and his appointment as colonel, but neither this nor the arrival of additional Virginians along with an independent company of South Carolinians commanded by a cooperative Captain James Mackay cheered him. Supplies were always uncertain and his Indian allies were becoming more and more fainthearted. The Iroquois Council had ordered their dependent tribes to be neutral, and the Half-King was understandably concerned about defying his overlords by staying with a loser. Assessing their situation, a council of officers on June 28 advised the colonel to pull back to Wills Creek. Low supplies, inadequate transport, and the exhaustion of the men meant that even this could not be done quickly, and while Washington prepared for the withdrawal the Half-King considered his alternatives and, sometime during the night of July 2, he and his warriors left. The delay did not worry the young commander as he was quite proud of his fort, but it was actually poorly sited, within musket shot of the woods, and too small for the force he had; it well deserved the Half-King's derisive description as "that little thing upon the Meadow."[9]

The Indians had not gotten away a moment too soon. As the morning of July 3 came, gray with the promise of rain, French scouts were seen in the neighborhood. By noon the fort was surrounded and under fire from the forest. The rain and the gunfire continued through the day, with the defenders being able to make little reply. By nightfall, the powder wet, the men weary, and, having broken into the rum supply, becoming undisciplined, resistance was almost at an end. From the darkness a shouted "Voulez vous parler?" was heard and refused, but a second offer to treat outside the fort was accepted. There the Virginians' interpreter, Adam VanBraam, working from a smudged copy, by a guttering candle in the rainy night, explained the surprisingly moderate French terms. The enemy commander was having trouble with his own Indians and supplies and feared the imminent arrival of enemy reinforcements; thus a quick surrender was as advantageous for the French as it was necessary for Washington. But hidden in the capitulation agreement was a statement that Jumonville's "assassination" had been by Washington's party; VanBraam mistranslated this as death. The colonel's signature on the agreement was a virtual admission that he was a murderer, and the French later made much of this when they issued a statement justifying the resumption of hostilities.[10]

Washington managed to bring about 165 of his force of 400 back to Wills Creek, most of the losses being caused by desertion. Although the first verdict on Washington's command was favorable and sympathetic, it was soon qualified and he was accused of impetuosity and disobedience to orders, among other things. Few of the charges had much substance; his orders, for example, were vague and left much to his judgment; whether or not he disobeyed them is a moot point. Impetuosity was a fair enough charge, but what should Dinwiddie have expected from an inexperienced officer eager to prove himself in his first command? As a person and as an officer, caution and circumspection developed slowly in Washington and only as the result of strenuous self-discipline. The basic problem in the Fort Necessity campaign was the lack of men and supplies. Virginia alone could not throw back the French, as she tried to do in 1754; in some respects the campaign was a miniature rehearsal of what Washington would have to endure later during the War for Independence. On his return to Williamsburg, the colonel discovered that Dinwiddie had decided to break up the regiment into ten companies, with no officer higher than a captain. Washington angrily refused the offer of one of the captaincies and resigned his commission in October. His first attempt to "push his fortune in the Military Way" had come to an end.

But he had not given up, and, while resting at Belvoir, interesting rumors were circulating around the colony, rumors that were soon confirmed. A new expedition was to be sent against the Forks, organized around a core of English regulars commanded by General James Braddock. The general arrived at Alexandria in February 1755 and Washington lost no time in making himself known, sending a rather unctuous congratulatory note assuring Braddock that the French would presently be pushed out of the Ohio Valley. Partly because of this but probably more because of Dinwiddie's recommendation, Washington was invited to go along as a volunteer aide on Braddock's staff. He hesitated, balancing the costs of his neglect of Mount Vernon against the benefits of a possible royal commission issued on the recommendation of a successful general. Hope won out over practical considerations and he accepted. Mount Vernon was left in the care of his younger brother John Augustine ("Jack") and he joined Braddock at Frederick, Maryland, early in May.

Braddock was already experiencing the frustration that his new aide had experienced the year before. The truth seems to have been that, even with all the guineas in the world, Virginia's economy was too oriented toward the production of tobacco and its settlement too dispersed to serve as a supply base for a large military force. The wild, mountainous terrain between Frederick and the Forks only magnified the supply problem. Braddock could cover only a little more than two miles a day and consulted with Washington on how things might be speeded up. The Virginian suggested splitting the force in two; one unit with most of the infantry would move ahead, relieved of the baggage and heavy artillery, which would come on behind. Braddock accepted the advice in the hope of blocking the advance of French reinforcements to the Forks. Unfortunately for him, Washington was sick with typhoid and had to stay with the second unit until he recovered.

By July 8 Washington had joined the first unit, which was only twelve miles from the Forks. Early the next morning the men set out on what they expected to be their last day of marching—for too many of them it was their last day. A tricky double crossing of the winding Monongahela was pulled off successfully and the way seemed clear to the Forks. Braddock ordered the band to play "The Grenadier's March" and the redcoats moved through the forest almost as if it were Hyde Park. But the general was no fool, and flankers and an advance party guarded the main force. All this meant nothing as, shortly before noon, the advance party was surprised by a mixed force of French and Indians who themselves had not expected to find the English so close to the Forks. The hurried retreat of the advance men threw the main body into confusion and they were unable to prevent themselves from being surrounded by the more adaptable enemy. The English were now in a sunken path through a thick forest and receiving heavy fire from the hidden enemy. The men began to bunch up in the center of the path and fire their muskets indiscriminately; when the officers tried to form them into lines and start them toward the enemy, they refused to leave the specious safety of the open area. Trained for an entirely different kind of fighting, the redcoats were at a serious disadvantage and soon panicked. Washington and the other officers were prime targets; near the end of the battle Braddock took a ball through his lungs but the Virginian was luckier. Although he lost two horses and several shots went through his clothes, he survived the day unscathed. This was the purest luck or perhaps Providence, for he behaved with "the greatest courage and resolution."

More than courage was needed as the retreat degenerated into a rout. After discipline was restored, Washington was sent to get help from the second unit. Through the night he moved slowly through the almost impenetrable darkness, occasionally falling over wounded men who had fled the action, to find Colonel Thomas Dunbar already aware of the defeat and ready to move forward. The division of the force had been especially fortunate, as it gave the remnants of the first unit a nearby refuge, albeit a temporary one. Reforming his units, Braddock discovered he had lost 977 of the 1,459 men he had taken forward with him. Late on the night of July 13 another figure was added to the casualty list when the general himself died. Courageous but obstinate, a solid, conventional tactician, he was the wrong man in a task for which there was, quite possibly, no right man. Three days after his general's death, Colonel Dunbar brought the survivors into Fort Cumberland and prepared them for the march to Philadelphia and winter quarters.

There were a good many mistakes in the expedition, but Washington fastened on the unexpected time and place of the battle. Braddock expected trouble at the Monongahela fords; once past them he assumed the expedition would not be molested until it reached the Forks. For their part, the French had wanted to hit the English at the fords but had been delayed by trouble with the Indians; they were hurrying toward the fords when they encountered the redcoats. When the shooting began, "Victory was their [the French] smallest expectation," as Washington put it. The quick flexibility of the French and Indians and the unfamiliarity of the English with the forest setting and proper tactics almost dictated the outcome of the battle. Washington had gotten a valuable lesson on the virtues of adaptability. Before the end of July he was convalescing at Mount Vernon from his typhoid and the exertions of the campaign.[11]

Dunbar's withdrawal left Virginia defenseless, and Governor Dinwiddie had no alternative but to ask the Burgesses once again to tap the colony's resources. They responded quickly and, for the time being, generously, with £ 40,000 to support a regiment of 1,000 soldiers and several companies of rangers. Although Washington had come to regret the cost of his earlier service to Virginia, he could not refuse the colonelcy of the new regiment if it was offered as it was equivalent to his old position. The Stoic concept of duty dictated that if the post were "offer'd upon such terms as can't be objected against, it wou'd reflect eternal dishonor upon me to refuse it." For all his sincere concern about duty and honor, Washington nevertheless made certain the terms could not be "objected against" before he accepted Dinwiddie's offer of a provincial colonelcy in August 1755, securing increased pay and control of the selection of officers.

The colonel began his duties with a flurry of activity that reflected the urgency of his task and the accuracy of Dinwiddie's description of him as "a man of great merit and resolution." But more than good character was going to be needed to defend a frontier several hundred miles long against roving bands of Indians. Soon, as Washington remembered it:

the frontiers were continually harassed, but not having enough force to carry the war [to the Forks], he could do no more than distribute the Troops along the Frontiers in the Stockaded Forts; more with a view to quiet the fears of the Inhabitants than from any expectation of giving securities in so extensive a line to the settlements. [12]

The only false note here is Washington's apparent acquiescence; he acquiesced in nothing and worked almost without rest to deploy the inadequate resources he had for his task. The frontiersmen tended to panic at the least sign of Indians; the militia were reluctant to turn out, even when their families were safe in protected settlements; impressment of men and supplies brought threats of violence against the colonel; and few of his subordinates performed satisfactorily, throwing an even heavier burden on the commander. He was not able to see the humor of a panic in Winchester caused, personal investigation by Washington disclosed, by "3 drunken Soldiers of the Light-Horse," drinking and firing their muskets in a clearing near the town. The "raiding party" was marched off to the guardhouse to sober up. Dinwiddie responded to the colonel's endless requests for more support with endless requests to the Burgesses while he counseled the younger man to be patient and to persist. Unfortunately for both the governor and the colonel the Burgesses, after their initial appropriation, supported the regiment grudgingly, making a difficult task practically impossible. To Washington, acutely eager for public esteem and anxious about the effect of the unit's poor performance on his reputation, the frustrations of command were severe, causing him to be unreasonably demanding of the governor, whose situation was almost as frustrating as his own, and to grasp eagerly at a royal commission as if it were a magic talisman which would instantly cure all his problems.

The pride and insecurity of the young officer were clearly seen when he encountered Captain John Dagworthy, who had once possessed a royal commission, in command of a Maryland force at Fort Cumberland. Dagworthy claimed precedence over Washington because of his royal commission, and, when the colonel could not talk Dagworthy out of the claim, Washington simply stayed away from Cumberland, even recommending to Dinwiddie that Virginia abandon the fort despite its obvious utility. Throughout the quarrel, Dinwiddie loyally supported Washington, even permitting him to go to Boston in February–March 1756 to get a ruling on the matter from Governor William Shirley, the commander-in-chief of His Majesty's forces in North America. Shirley's decision did not settle the matter and Washington continued to avoid the fort, even disobeying a direct order from Dinwiddie. The governor forgave this and again permitted Washington a furlough, this time to carry his case to New York and Lord Loudoun, the new commander-in-chief. In presenting his position to Loudoun in the spring of 1757, the colonel styled himself "free from guile," but he nevertheless accompanied a request for royal commissions for himself and his officers with a description of Dinwiddie as obstructive and interfering, hardly a fair verdict. Washington was so anxious about his own reputation and eager for a royal commission that he could not see the situation clearly enough to do justice to his immediate superior. And Loudoun ignored the petition. Fortunately for both men, Dinwiddie returned to England in 1757, leaving Washington to work things out with his successor.

Almost coincidental with Dinwiddie's retirement, the king's new chief minister, William Pitt, ordered an offensive in North America in 1758 which aimed at several strategic points, including the Forks of the Ohio, where the French had built Fort Duquesne. Using Philadelphia as his base, Brigadier-General John Forbes was to command the effort against the Forks. Virginia's new governor, Francis Fauquier, received authorization for a second regiment from the Burgesses along with permission for both regiments to go outside the colony. For once things went smoothly and Washington and his colleague Colonel William Byrd, III, took almost 2,000 men into the field with Washington as a courtesy "Brigadier" at their head. Adequately supported and under a skilled and successful commander, Washington's desire to "be distinguished in some measure from the *common run* [orig. emph.] of provincial officers" seemed about to be satisfied.

The expedition began well, with Forbes and his subordinate, Colonel Henry Bouquet, consulting the provincial officers and adopting some of their suggestions, including Washington's idea of hunting shirts and leggings as a suitable uniform for the wild. But the possibility of dissension was there from the beginning. Forbes was to cut a road as he went, expecting peacetime civilian traffic to follow it; both Pennsylvania and Virginia wanted it inside their borders. Starting from Philadelphia, Forbes was predisposed to push straight across Pennsylvania, but the Virginians pushed strongly to bend the road south at Raystown so it would meet Braddock's old road at Cumberland. Although longer, they argued it would be faster than building a new road. Forbes was no fool; he was well aware of the provincial rivalry and discounted both sides' arguments. Delay did not frighten him as the English were already working on the Indians elsewhere with diplomacy (and gifts) and the coming of winter always made the savages eager to return to their villages and prepare for cold weather; time only improved the chances of both these factors. Finally, other English forces were moving against other French posts; the success of any of them would weaken the French position at Duquesne. None of this seemed significant to Washington as he persistently pushed Braddock's road as the only reasonable choice. Even after Forbes had decided to push straight across from Raystown, Washington hinted darkly that he and Bouquet were the 'd[u]pes, or something worse to P[enn]s[yl]v[ania]n Artifice." And his prophecy of disaster should the force not use Braddock's road seemed about to come true as the expedition apparently bogged down in mid-November, still about fifty miles from Duquesne. But intelligence came, via a French deserter, that Duquesne was weakly manned and the French had been deserted by their Indian allies. Twenty-five hundred men, Washington's regiment among them, were sent forward on a reconnaisance; they found Duquesne burned and deserted. By the end of November, the Forks were in English hands. Washington did not understand how Forbes had succeeded where Braddock had failed and claimed that the "possession of this fort has been a matter of great surprise to the whole army," a statement Forbes would have resented had he seen it. The English general's slow, steady advance while the factors mentioned above were working had pushed the French away from the Forks with no more luck than is commonly found in human affairs.[13]

The colonial troops were sent back to their respective colonies except for a small unit of Virginians assigned to garrison "Fort Pitt" over the winter while Forbes took his Scottish Highlanders, the only regulars in the expedition, back to Philadelphia. While riding through the now-familiar country between Fort Pitt and Williamsburg, Washington must frequently have mulled over his recent experiences and reaffirmed the decision which he had made unconsciously before the campaign had begun. As his imprudent support of Braddock's road had shown, he was now putting provincial concerns ahead of his desire for a royal commission; why else would he antagonize Forbes by so assiduously pushing Virginia's interest? He was going to resign his commission, return to Mount Vernon, and tend to his lands. The attempt to push his "Fortune in the Military Way" was at an end.

CHAPTER 2

Gentleman, Planter, and Rebel, 1758–1775

I am now, I believe, fixed at this seat with an agreeable consort for life, and hope to find more happiness in retirement that I ever experienced amidst a wide and bustling World.

THE former colonel had not returned to Mount Vernon to sulk; there was far too much to do. He was in love and about to be married, although not to the same woman. Sometime in the spring of 1758, his proposal was accepted by Martha Dandridge Custis, an attractive widow with two children. Yet in September he was writing tortured, involved love letters to George William Fairfax's wife, Sally, the reigning mistress of Belvoir. While away with Forbes, Washington wrote at least two letters to Sally in which he, indirectly but clearly, told her he loved her and asked her to declare whether or not she felt the same. She seems to have returned joking responses (they have been lost) in which she avoided an answer. But he was not to be put off and declared he would be far happier playing "Juba to such a Marcia as you must make." These were a pair of lovers from Joseph Addison's *Cato*, a play much liked by Washington and frequently quoted by him. His love for Sally Fairfax, the wife of one of his closest friends, was a strong and almost certainly unrequited feeling which had developed unnoticed during his many happy visits to Belvoir. But as long as George William lived, it would go no further. As Samuel Eliot Morison has commented; "It was a situation that schooled the young soldier-lover in manners, moderation, and restraint—a test case of his Stoical philosophy." The letters were a last attempt to get a declaration of his feelings from Sally, who may well have been frightened of the tall soldier who was obviously controlling his feelings only with difficulty. But he did control them, showing the self-discipline which would be so notable in his fully

30

developed character; he would not allow an involuntary emotion to consume his and his friends' happiness.[1]

His affection for Martha was, as the quotation heading this chapter indicates, not the same as he felt for Sally. But his marriage was not strictly one of convenience. Both husband and wife began their union with a high regard for one another which matured into a quiet and deep love, a love which calmed and nourished both. Mrs. Custis was also a widow with a large estate to administer and two children to raise; she was probably as glad to hand the properties over to her new husband as he was pleased to have a wife to grace—and to run—the house at Mount Vernon. The marriage certainly had elements of convenience for both parties. The colonel and his lady made a contrasting couple; Washington was more than six feet tall, reasonably slim at 175 pounds, while Martha was just over five feet tall and amiably described herself as plump. While his general build was large-boned, she was petite, and while his demeanor was "at all times composed and dignified," she was smiling and chatty. It was more a study in complementary attributes than opposites.[2]

Washington's lands had been neglected, despite the stewardship of his brother, because the Mount Vernon soil was poor and required very close attention before any return was secured. The livestock were also run down and more slaves were needed to work the land; buildings had to be built and provisions purchased, "and other matters, which swallowed up, well before I knew where I was, all the money got by Marriage, nay more, brought me into debt." Washington would remain in debt until 1773 when his step-daughter died and he inherited the child's estate, more than enough to balance the debit owed the London firm he corresponded with. But this would be the culmination of a process he had begun in 1760 when he began to improve Mount Vernon. It then consisted of 5,518 acres; further purchases would increase it to 8,000 acres. He also owned Ferry Farm, but his mother lived there and took its income and some 7,000 acres in the Piedmont and the Shenandoah Valley, none of it especially valuable then.[3] All in all, it was a slim enough base on which to build, but, with hard work and systematic management, it would do.

Not only the farms needed expansion; the Mount Vernon "mansion" was actually a cramped story-and-a-half farmhouse; first, a second floor was added and then, before and after the War for Independence, wings on either end, along with the portico which gave the building its familiar outline. Washington designed these additions and also took charge of the house's interior decoration; the finished product was very much a reflection of his taste and personality, a formal and reserved building for a master with much the same characteristics. Both by necessity—long distances and few taverns—and custom, Virginians entertained each other frequently and Washington was true to the tradition; between 1768 and 1775, he and Martha had about 2,000 dinner guests, most of them for at least one night. Few Washingtons were among them; they were seen at their own homes or in Williamsburg. Most of the guests were friends and neighbors—George Mason of Gunston Hall, just the other side of Belvoir, and of course the Fairfaxes, along with some of Martha's family. Mary Washington never came to Mount Vernon after Martha became its mistress. Conventional in his entertaining, he was also conventional in his sports, riding to the hounds, duck-shooting and card-playing. But here his urge to keep records surfaced and in January 1775 he carefully calculated his winnings and losses for the last three years and soberly entered a debit of £6.3.3, "By. Balc^e against Play"; indulge himself he would, but not to the point of extravagance.[4]

Nor would he be extravagant in the objects with which he surrounded himself; in his orders to Robert Cary and Company, his London consignees, he constantly emphasized three qualities: good, neat, and, where applicable, fashionable but not ostentatious. Like many Virginians he was frequently disappointed by what he received and often complained that the goods were "mean in quality but not in price, for in this they excel." Despite the usual difficulties, the appurtenances of a gentleman's house were gradually accumulated, including a library of several hundred books, strong in history and agricultural and legal manuals. In 1772 he and Martha were painted by the noted portraitist Charles Willson Peale. Clad in his uniform, Washington looks out with a grave, studied, and unrevealing expression, fulfilling the subject's prophecy that "the skill of this Gentleman's Pencil, will be put to it in describing to the World what manner of Man I am." Peale did not succeed, and few who followed him did much better.

Himself personally abstemious, Washington nevertheless took people pretty much as he found them. In 1787 he hired a gardener, obviously a heavy drinker, and provided in the contract that the man, in return for daily sobriety, would receive so many dollars to be drunk for a specified number of days at each holiday. When he headed the regiment, his instructions to his officers were often filled with injunctions against excessive drinking and sexual indulgence, but these were always linked with the performance of their duties, not with moral strictures. He seems to have lacked a personal religious faith; when he referred to a force which initiated and, to an extent, controlled life, he always vaguely called it Providence or another unrevealing term. The Anglican Church of colonial Virginia had almost entirely lost sight of its religious goals and become simply one of the institutions which helped to govern the colony. Washington's membership in the local parish and its vestry was just another of the duties expected of a planter and not a sign of a religious faith. He was much more constant in his attendance at vestry meetings, which had secular duties in addition to running the parish, than he was at Sunday services; it is easy to see which form of service had priority in Washington's mind. [5]

"Everywhere order, method, punctuality, economy reigned." Thus runs the idyllic remembrance of George Washington Parke Custis, Martha's grandson, of his boyhood at Mount Vernon in the 1780s. However true it might have been then, it can be taken only as a goal for the Mount Vernon of the 1760s. Although its owner entered into his command of his "people" and his cultivation of his acres in the same systematic, conscientious manner he had run the regiment, slaves and tobacco proved to be as uncooperative as enlisted men and the French and Indians had been. But ingenuity and a willingness to experiment enabled him to make Mount Vernon profitable.

Washington began by vowing to grow the best Virginia tobacco possible, premium leaf for which he would receive premium prices, but he soon realized his soil would not permit this. He did increase substantially the quantity, but the quality was always poor. In debt as he was, he needed a cash crop; most Virginia planters would have stayed with tobacco to the final, unprofitable end. But as early as 1760 he was experimenting with different grasses and grains, some unknown to local planters. By 1763 he was ready to sign a contract with an Alexandria firm to take all his wheat at 3s. 9d. a bushel; within seven years they were receiving more than 6,000 bushels a year from him. In 1770 his own mill began to turn his wheat into flour, and he could export directly from his wharf on the Potomac, also the source of fish, dried and packed for additional income and also fed to the slaves. Yields from the livestock, especially sheep for wool, helped to increase his income further. Painstaking attention to his fields and a willingness to try unusual crops plus a conscious attempt to cut down purchases from London and a resolve to purchase no more slaves combined to decrease substantially his debt and increase the value of Mount Vernon. Still and all, it was only an inheritance from his stepdaughter, Martha Custis, which wiped out the debt in London. Despite this qualification, the steady decrease in debt and the increase in marketable produce brought about by Washington when contrasted with the growth in debt and the decrease in cash crops owing to poor cultivation and soil exhaustion common to most other Virginia planters make his achievement creditable if not unique. Further, the problems of supply, inadequate resources, supervising unwilling slaves and incompetent or irresponsible overseers, relating all aspects of the plantation's operation to the twin goals of supporting his family and getting himself out of debt were a suitable, albeit unconscious, preparation for the problems of command he would encounter during the War for American Independence. Just as the command of the Virginia Regiment had helped to prepare him for the challenge of turning Mount Vernon into a profitable enterprise, so too its demands were strengthening him for his next great task. [6]

Although Washington was certainly gratified at the steady gains realized at Mount Vernon, his hopes for gaining a fortune were not based on it. He once observed to a ne'er-do-well neighbor that all the great fortunes in the province had been obtained by securing large tracts of land on the fringes of settlement and beyond and then waiting for it to appreciate. That he practiced what he preached to Captain Posey could be seen with his first purchase in the Shenandoah; now he proposed to begin gathering in acres in earnest. Even before the end of the war, he inquired of Virginia's governor about the honoring of a 1754 land bounty proclaimed by Governor Dinwiddie, but the Proclamation of 1763 signified the Crown's decision to postpone western settlement until it could puzzle out the proper policy to follow. This did not lessen Washington's interest, and he took advantage of the enforced delay to spy out choice tracts, but it had to be done quietly lest

it might give the alarm to others and, by putting them upon a plan of the same nature . . . set the different Interests aclashing, and probably in the end overturn the whole; all which may be avoided by a Silent management. . . .

Washington's expectation of a quick reopening of the West was correct; Indian treaties in 1767 cleared an extensive area. The former colonel now had three opportunities to gather in Western land: 1) the 1754 Dinwiddie bounty; 2) a 1763 bounty to all those who served until the end of the war; 3) land vouchers purchased from Indian traders indemnified for losses in Pontiac's Rebellion. Of the three the Dinwiddie bounty could be handled within the colony, and Washington organized a committee in 1769 to secure its redemption. A trip west in the fall of 1770 permitted Washington to select a peninsula formed by the Ohio and Great Kanawha rivers as the most suitable site, and surveying began. At the end of the process, Washington had received 20,147 of the 200,000 acres of the bounty, but his land was concentrated along the river bottoms, the most accessible and the most fertile portion of the tract, "the cream of the Country," as he later described it. Considering that the language of the original proclamation strongly suggests that it was confined to the enlisted men and that Virginia law forbade engrossing the bottom lands to the extent Washington had, his conduct verged on, if it did not move into, the unethical. And every acre he took meant one less for the enlisted men, who received only 400 acres each.

Although Washington was clearly ineligible for the 1763 bounty, his participation hurt no one else as the land was taken from the almost illimitable Crown lands, a cow already well milked by many other Virginians with much less justification than Washington, who had suffered losses because of his military service. He received a colonel's share, 5,000 acres, and purchased—secretly, to keep the price low—the shares of others who did not care to redeem them. Several thousand more acres in western Pennsylvania were secured with the Indian traders' vouchers. All in all, he had secured 33,000 acres, not always by creditable méans, but all at minimum or no cost. [7]

Curiously, Washington's vision of the future development of the West, although he recognized its importance, both economic and political, was backward-looking, not forward. He was so concerned with providing a sure income that he thought only of settling his lands with leaseholders or indentured servants, not freeholders; the land was to stay with the Washingtons and not to be sold. While waiting for willing tenants he began a farm, to be worked by indentured servants, on the Great Kanawha, but this work was interrupted by the War for Independence and never resumed. The war also interrupted another project Washington recognized as important to the development of the country. In 1770 he responded eagerly to a proposal of Governor Thomas Johnson of Maryland that Virginia cooperate in improving the navigation of the Potomac. The modest plan soon developed into a project to build a canal to Cumberland where land transport would have to take over. Although Maryland did not act,

Virginia did charter a canal company in 1772, and some work was done before the War began.[8]

Although Washington never received the great riches he hoped for from his western lands, in a sense the United States did. His acres on the Ohio reinforced his already strong interest in the West and in the creation of effective ties of commerce and economic interest across the mountains. In 1772 these ties were meant to bind Virginia together; later they helped to tie together a nation. That Washington could later evolve from a Virginia provincial into an American nationalist was due, to an extent, to these bounty lands.

Although Mount Vernon provided full-time occupation, Washington's membership in the Virginia gentry meant that he had to take up other unofficial—and unpaid—duties; county government was conducted almost entirely by planters through their membership on vestries and service as justices of the peace, to which position Washington was appointed in 1770. They also looked after the poor of the neighborhood, within and without the system of the poor laws, lent money, and cosigned each other's notes. One of the most burdensome duties that fell unofficially to them was executing wills for friends' widows and orphans; although Washington tried to avoid this, he could never bring himself to refuse flatly and at one point was the executor for five separate estates. Time-consuming as such duties were, they were still welcome signs of his membership in the gentry and his reputation for integrity and trustworthiness among his peers.

The political system within which Washington worked, while not democratic in the modern definition, did reflect the popular will to a substantial degree and depended upon popular support which was invited, not coerced. Although there were both built-in and customary advantages for the wealthy in the system, ordinary men could and did vote in Burgess elections which were as much social occasions as exercises of the franchise. The fact that planters held a near monopoly of government positions reflected both the deference which the middling and lower orders paid their superiors and the concentration in the gentry of those whose native talents were sufficiently developed to make them effective legislators. Although Washington thought of seeking election to the Burgesses as early as 1755, it was not until December 1756 that his name was put forward, at the last minute, at the Frederick County election; he finished third in a field of three. With more planning and a sounding-out of the local notables, all of whom supported him, he secured election in July 1758 for Frederick; in 1765 a vacancy opened in Fairfax County, where Mount

Vernon was, and he transferred his political base to that county. In the Burgesses, the colonel was not one of the leaders. His distaste for public speaking and a growing habit of thinking long and hard before coming to a decision, a sign of his success in disciplining the strong feelings he had too often vented on Dinwiddie, kept him from speaking casually and quickly. As Jefferson later noted, Washington shared with Benjamin Franklin a habit of speaking briefly and only to "the main point which was to decide the question." During his Burgess terms, he was content to be an inconspicuous though useful member, and one has to look elsewhere to see how he felt about the developing crisis in imperial relations between England and her North American colonies. [9]

Washington's first reaction to this crisis centered on the Stamp Act, passed by the Parliament in March 1765 and levying a tax, to be paid in scarce coin, on practically every kind of printed document used in the colonies. The act inspired the first intercolonial meeting held under American auspices, the Stamp Act Congress, which met in New York in October. Virginia was not represented there as the Burgesses were not in session to appoint a delegation. Washington's attention was focused on the nonimportation schemes already adopted by several colonies. He felt that while such schemes could only hurt England, they could only benefit the colonies by encouraging self-sufficiency; "this consequently will introduce frugality and be a necessary stimulation to industry." His strongest reference to the act was to call it "an Act of Oppression," as anyone who viewed it properly could see; but throughout the crisis, which ended with the act's repeal in March 1766, Washington saw it as a goad to local self-sufficiency, a goal he was ready to abandon if England would act justly toward the colonies. He does not seem to have been concerned very much with the constitutional aspect of the controversy, being content to view it within the parochial framework of his own and Virginia's interests.

Nor did the next round of contention with England shake him quickly from his apparent unconcern. In 1767, when the Parliament levied the Townshend Duties on certain goods imported into the colonies, he skipped the session of the Burgesses which passed a vigorous protest. Even his involvement in Virginia's resistance shows how unfamiliar he was with the actively anti-English policy; when a friend sent him the text of a proposed antiimportation agreement he copied it and sent it to his neighbor George Mason, the agreement's author. However belated, his feelings, once aroused, were strong; to him the only question was how to stop "our lordly masters" from subverting Virginia's liberty. He would not "scruple or hesitate to use a[r]ms in defense of so valuable a blessing," but that would have to be a last resort. Even in his anger he went out of his way to point out the economic advantages to Virginia in cutting down the debt owed to English merchants and encouraging local manufactures. In May 1769 he took a copy of the agreement to the Burgesses' session; however, before it could be adopted Governor Botetourt dissolved the House for anti-Crown resolutions. This did not stop the Burgesses, meeting as "the principal Gentlemen of the Colony," from adopting the report of a committee, of which Washington was a member, incorporating the principal features of his and Mason's agreement. His usual posture of passive involvement had obviously been set aside. The informal meeting adjourned on May 18 and Washington headed home to muster Fairfax County behind the "Association," as the agreement had been dubbed. Although Washington claimed it worked well in Fairfax, this was not true of Virginia (or Maryland) generally, and the nonimportation movement petered out after Parliament repealed all the Townshend Duties except one on tea in 1770. Despite his active support of the Association, Washington was far from being a rebel. His objections were to specific acts; he would have to see evidence of a consistent plan to subvert Virginia's liberties before he could support anything more drastic than the nonimportation agreements. Such evidence was soon forthcoming.

Ironically, the act which provided the "evidence" was not intended to change the imperial relationship but rather to aid the perennially ailing East India Company by giving it a monopoly on the lucrative American tea market and remitting all the duties paid on its tea except the Townshend duty, kept specifically as an assertion of Parliament's right to tax the colonies. Despite this, the legislation was passed with little thought as to its effect in America. But the effect was immediate and vigorous. Up and down the coast merchants and people cooperated in refusing the dutied tea; faced with the strong reaction, royal governors usually capitulated. Only in Boston did push come to shove when Governor Thomas Hutchison insisted in enforcing the act against the obdurate resistance of the local Sons of Liberty. The Boston Tea Party, December 16, 1773, resolved the conflict, but only at the cost of punitive legislation from a retaliating Parliament. The "Intolerable" or "Coercive" Acts changed the form of Massachusetts government, closed the port of Boston, and strengthened the authority of crown officials throughout the colonies as well as requiring a closer compliance with the Quartering Act. The Parliament's expectation that Massachusetts would find itself isolated was sorely disappointed. The other colonies immediately supported their stricken sister.[10]

Washington cooperated fully with Virginia's condemnation of the Coercive Acts and call for a general meeting of the colonies. Although he disapproved of the tea's destruction, he affirmed to George William Fairfax that "the cause of Boston . . . now is and ever will be considered as the cause of America" and regretted that Virginia, concerned over a possible Indian war, should find the English government trying "by every piece of Art and despotism to fix the Shackles of Slavery upon us." Cooperating with Mason in a local call for nonimportation, the idea was put forward that the people could be bound only by the actions of their own representatives, a right of all Englishmen. The call was adopted at county meetings in July 1774, which also reelected Washington one of the Fairfax County Burgesses. By now he had all the proof he needed to see "a fixed and uniform plan to tax us." To the assertion that more petitions to the Crown should be sent, he exploded that England had already been told Americans would not accept their taxes; "what reason is there to expect anything from their justice?" The Americans were contending for the right of self-taxation and, "as Englishmen, we could not be deprived of this essential and valuable part of a constitution." "An innate spirit of freedom" had first told him that England's policy was contrary to "natural justice." Others had shown him that it was also contrary to the English constitution and Virginia's charter. A line had to be drawn between England's power and Virginia's rights; he wished the time for drawing it had not come during his lifetime,

but the crisis is arrived when we must assert our rights, or submit to every imposition that can be heaped upon us, till custom and use shall make us as tame and abject slaves, as the blacks we rule over with such arbitrary sway.

Clearly Washington had reached a point from which there could be no return. Unless England changed her colonial policy, steps more drastic and far-reaching than nonimportation would have to be taken. Although independence had not yet occurred to him, it was a logical conclusion to what he had already written.

In August an extralegal meeting of Burgesses convened in Williamsburg and called for a general meeting of the colonies, suggesting that the congress urge a nonimportation, nonexportation agreement similar to Virginia's, and counseled the diversification of the colony's agriculture and the encouragement of manufacturing (old ideas of Washington's) and the easing of trade regulations. Seven Burgesses, including Washington, were chosen to represent Virginia at the general meeting, scheduled for Philadelphia in September. Washington had come to his present position entirely out of concern for Virginia; now, meeting and talking with men from other colonies, he could begin to appreciate their differing desires and needs.

By September 5 Washington and a sufficient number of other delegates were in Philadelphia to convene what was soon formally titled the Continental Congress. In the Congress's organization and deliberation, Washington presumably took a part, but that part is not known. He kept only a bare-bones diary of where and with whom he ate, served on no committees, and was mentioned only glancingly by those who noticed him. Silas Deane of Connecticut approved his "easy, soldier like air and gesture" and was surprised at his youthful appearance; but he also repeated the apocryphal story of the Virginian's offer to raise and support a regiment, commenting cautiously, "His fortune is said to be equal to such an undertaking." Getting back to safer ground, he noted that Washington spoke "very modestly and in a cool but determined style and accent." Another Yankee, Rhode Islander Solomon Drowne, went beyond fair taste when he sent home a verse which concluded: ". . . With manly gait/His faithful steel suspended by his side,/Pass'd W-shi-gt-n along, Virginia's hero," adding a daydream in which the imperial quarrel was settled by George III and George of Mount Vernon in personal combat! More accurately, Washington described himself at the Congress as "an attentive observer and witness."[11]

While the Congress debated—and rejected—a plan of union with England and approved a firm and spirited defense of colonial rights, Washington's perception of the situation deepened and, to an extent, changed. After a dinner with the leading men of New England, he denied that they, or any American, wanted independence, his first recorded mention of that definitive step. But he did assert that no Yankee, or American, would "ever submit to the loss of those valuable rights and privileges, which are essential to the happiness of every free state, and without which life, liberty, and property are rendered totally insecure." No one wanted war, but if England refused to back down, "more blood will be spilt on this occasion . . . than history has yet furnished instances of in North America."

Congress's position, gleaned from its statements, was moderate enough. They would not accept English taxation or interference with their internal government, especially interference with personal rights long thought guaranteed by the English constitution, but they would accept legitimate regulation of their trade for imperial interests. No mention was made of armed resistance, but such thoughts must have occurred to the delegates, as Deane and Drowne's comments attest. They also occurred to Washington's mind, for, among his purchases in Philadelphia, was a work on military discipline. Perhaps a new opportunity to "push his Fortune in a Military Way" was in the future?[12]

Washington returned to Mount Vernon at the end of October. His five weeks in Philadelphia had enlarged his acquaintances, giving him his first glimpse of several of those with whom his future career would be inextricably bound, John Adams, John Jay, Joseph Reed, and Thomas Mifflin, to name only a few of the famous and not so famous who would figure in the struggle for independence. Although he had played a passive and obscure role, he had certainly been observed. Had he gone to the colonial metropolis for the first time in 1775 when the second Congress convened, with many of the same men who had been there seven months before, would the opportunity given to him then been given at all?

CHAPTER 3

In the Service of Congress, 1775–1783

The sword was to be forged upon the anvil of necessity.

AFTER his service in the Congress, Washington's life in Virginia never returned to what he considered normal. Added to his already busy life was service on several committees whose task was to improve Virginia's military defenses. Although they were disguised in the language of loyal submission, these preparations made clear that many felt a resort to "a-ms" was becoming more and more likely. Certainly that was the feeling of Patrick Henry, who represented a western county at the second Virginia convention in March 1775 and who stirred the delegates with his famous rejection of more conciliatory petitions, concluding with: "I know not what course others may take; but as for me, give me liberty or give me death!" Descending from the grandiloqent level of Henry's oration, Washington received several more committee assignments at the meeting and, most important, he was again selected to represent his colony at the second Congress to be held in Philadelphia in May. He traveled north in a mood of sober resolution, having confided to his brother that it was his "full intention to devote my life and fortune in the cause we are engaged in, if need be." Virginia expected that his contribution would be military; as one anonymous rhymester put it: "In spite of Gage's flaming sword/And Carleton's Canadian troop/Brave Washington will give the word,/And we'll make them howl and whoop." Fortunately "Brave Washington" did not share the verse's mindless bravado.[1]

The trip to Philadelphia was filled with sober discussions of the repercussions of the encounters at Lexington and Concord the previous month. Once there, the delegates, a good many of whom had attended the previous meeting, got down to business quickly. All seemed to be "directed by the same firmness of union and determination to resist by all ways and to every extremity" English exactions. A

Massachusetts delegate saw the same feeling in Washington, that conciliation and compromise had been tried and found wanting, now the choice was between fighting or slavery. "Sad alternative! But can a virtuous man hesitate in the choice?" Implicitly, no.

While the Congress puzzled out what to do about the New England militia army which was besieging the English in Boston, Washington found himself on several military committees, but their work was aimless until the Congress came to a decision. There was only one decision they could make: New England had to be helped. And all that could be sent quickly to the aid of the Yankees was a symbol, a commander who would embody the decision of the Congress that this was America's, not New England's, cause. Washington was certainly aware that eyes were turning to him; his suitability was obvious on several counts. As a Virginian, he reassured the Yankees that they were not alone; further, his military experience and reputation made him a plausible candidate and his age—forty-three—and good health would help him bear the rigors of the position. On June 15, after a two-day debate, the Congress formally resolved that "a General be appointed to command all the continental forces, raised, or to be raised, for the defence of American liberty." Immediately, Thomas Johnson of Maryland placed Washington's name formally in nomination; no other nominations were made and the election was unanimous. The former Colonel of the Virginia Regiment had embarked "on a tempestuous ocean, from whence, perhaps, no friendly harbor is to be found."[2]

What manner of man had the Congress chosen to carry its standard against the "ministerial army"? The young Washington had a complex character; a combination of pride, ambition, and concern about his present and future status had pushed him forward into tasks from which less thrusting persons would have turned away. Fort LeBouef, Fort Necessity, the Braddock expedition, all were challenges which, if met well, could put aside any fears of inadequacy. But neither could he cut himself off from his Virginia roots, and he took on Mount Vernon even as he was resuming his military career. And it was essentially in Virginia's service that he spent three thankless years trying to do the impossible, defend the colony's frontier with always inadequate resources; this tried both his military ability and his character. He showed himself willing to work to the limit of his health and beyond, but he performed too many of the tasks which should have been left to subordinates. Although he, as was proper, took responsibility for the shortcomings of his officers and men, he was also too ready to take offense at slights, both real and imagined, and too conscious of the prerogatives of his rank. By the time of the Forbes expedition, he seems to have given up trying to secure a royal commission and actively sponsored, to his own detriment, Virginia's interests in the new military road. But the five years in the colony's service had taught him a good bit about himself, and now he brought his self-discipline, organizational ability, and capacity for hard work to the task of developing Mount Vernon. Here he also showed a readiness to break from established patterns and to admit failure and a realization of what he could and could not do. Only in the episode of the 1754 land bounty did his old anxiety about his fortune show itself.

As an adult, Washington was still a person of complex character. The pride, the readiness to take offense, the anxiety about his reputation—"honor," as the eighteenth century would call it—were present and had constantly to be restrained by his hard-bought self-discipline. Here he was helped by the secure place he had earned for himself; Colonel George Washington of Mount Vernon, Fairfax County, Virginia, need apologize to no one. Holder of a commission validated by years of service, owner of an extensive and profitable plantation, he was not living off the accumulated capital of his ancestors and pushing his estate deeper into debt by a mindless continuance of a timeworn agriculture on timeworn fields; respected as a man of prudence, judgment, and integrity in the county and in the colony, had it not been for the Revolution and the War for Independence he would have continued the busy, useful life he so enjoyed and would now forever lose.

When he accepted his appointment, Washington was, literally, *the* Continental Army, no men having been enlisted and no other officers appointed. Thus he became an instant symbol of the unswerving determination of the Congress to resist, at any price, English policy. As if he already realized this, he refused any salary for his services, asking only that his expenses, of which he would keep "an exact account," be paid. In resisting England, the Americans claimed to be defending eternal principles of liberty; Washington's conduct in his command would, as far as he was able, help to validate that claim. He would be charged with many faults during the war, but avarice would always be the least plausible.

Nor could he be plausibly charged with overconfidence. To the Congress he confessed that "I do not think myself equal to the Command I am honored with." He repeated this sentiment to

Martha, adding that he could not have refused "without exposing my character to such censure as would have reflected dishonor upon myself." Thus he moved to his new post, diffident of his own ability, confident that the cause was just and not quite understanding how its leadership had fallen to him. But lead it he would.

Although the Congress had more confidence than their general, they did not expect him to fight alone; in addition to providing for the enlistment of troops, they also appointed four major generals: Artemas Ward, then commanding the men around Boston; Charles Lee, an eccentric retired Royal Army officer; Philip Schuyler of New York; and Israel Putnam of Connecticut. Horatio Gates, another retired officer of the king, was appointed adjutant-general, and eight brigadiers, all but one from New England, were commissioned. Washington could appoint Continental officers up to colonel for the Continental service but the colonies would select their own militia officers. It was a less than ideal arrangement but the parochial jealousies of the colonies and the lack of congressional power made anything better unattainable. After recruiting two personable young Philadelphians, Joseph Reed and Thomas Mifflin, as secretaries, Washington left for the camp outside Boston.

He paused in New York City only long enough to receive the somewhat equivocal good wishes of its citizens (New York enjoyed—if that is the correct verb—a reputation for loyalty to the Crown) and to detach Philip Schuyler with a virtual carte blanche for the conduct of his command in upper New York. Although necessity dictated a loose rein on his detached subordinates, Washington had carelessly given up the right of the commander-in-chief to make all the truly important decisions; this carelessness would have important repercussions in the future.

The American headquarters at Cambridge was reached late on July 2 and Washington had his first glimpse of his new command; all in all, it was not too impressive. It took more than a week to secure an accurate count of the men—16,000 present, 14,000 fit for duty—but only a few minutes to realize that the army had no cannon or military engineers. One bright spot was an adequate supply of powder, 308 barrels, but even that was illusory and a month later Washington discovered that only thirty-six barrels were on hand; the higher amount was the total collected since Concord. The new general immediately began, in the fashion of new commanders, to tighten up his forces. All the militia was taken into the Continental Army on July

4; the general order announcing this prayed that "all distinctions of Colonies would be laid aside." But distinctions of rank were not, and officers were ordered to wear colored ribbons indicative of their status and some were separated from the service for various shortcomings. Because of a basic lack of supplies there were limits to what could be accomplished with the motley units besieging Boston, but Washington succeeded in bringing in a degree of order and regularity which was a pleasant contrast with what had been; William Emerson, minister of the Concord church, rejoiced at the "New lords new laws" which had wrought a surprising change, as early as the middle of July.[3]

With the army being brought into a degree of order, Washington began to wonder what to do with it. The Congress had ordered him to consult his generals; while the legislators had meant this for his guidance, Washington took it to be for his governance and went along with whatever the council of war decided, no matter how contrary to his own wishes the decision was. In the beginning this was good, as the new commander-in-chief was spoiling for a fight with the enemy which would bring the conflict to a quick end. This was at a time when the end would have been an American defeat. His first council of war advised simply a continuance of the siege while more troops were enlisted.

Washington was too active to rest content with such a passive attitude and looked for ways to annoy the English. He commissioned some converted merchantmen as privateers and sent them to intercept English supply ships bound for Boston. He also approved a two-pronged attack on Canada, one force under Brigadier-General James Montgomery moving up from New York; the other, under a short, swarthy, energetic officer from Connecticut, Benedict Arnold, would go through Maine. The official reason for this attack by the king's loyal subjects was to forestall an English-Indian attack from Canada. This ingenuous excuse underlines one of the main difficulties Washington faced at this time. Officially, the war was simply an effort to prevent an English force from enforcing obnoxious royal policies on otherwise loyal Americans. A Canadian invasion or taking the king's ships hardly fit in here. Washington and the Congress were finding out that there was no such thing as fighting a purely defensive war. Once the fighting had started, it became war, pure and simple. And once that had come about, independence was the next logical step. The siege of Boston, the Canadian expedition, Washington's little "navy," advice he gave to New England governors on Loyalists and other matters—together all these would constitute one of the major forces moving the Congress to declare "that these United Colonies are, and of right ought to be, free and independent."[4]

In September another council of war held Washington back from an attack on the English lines; their reasons were both military and political (a conciliatory proposal from Parliament was expected) but the general betrayed his eagerness to take the offensive when he reported the decision to the Congress. Later commentators have styled Washington a Fabian in his military strategy, that is, he set out to wear the enemy down in a series of small encounters which, even when they were American defeats, hurt the English sufficiently to take away their desire to continue the war, all with little risk to the Americans in any single encounter. Although it is true that he was frequently reduced to this, he never tired of planning a *coup de main* which would end the war by a single, overwhelming victory. In 1775–76, that would be the taking of Boston; after the loss of Manhattan, the retaking of that city would be Washington's objective. Thus, although circumspection, conservation, and caution often characterized his strategy, sometimes he had to be restrained from a daring gamble in which everything could be won—or lost. Fabian by necessity, he was a gambler by instinct.[5]

As the year ended, Washington had to abandon all thought of attack and bend every effort to keeping the army together. Practically all of the men had enlisted only to the year's end, and, although the Congress had optimistically authorized an army of more than 22,000, everyone soon discovered that authorization was one thing, enlistment was quite another; with six weeks to go, less than 1,000 men had reenlisted. Further, the reduction in the number of regiments meant some officers had to go and this had to be done without breaking provincial lines and putting a Rhode Islander in command of Connecticut troops. Washington almost despaired at the "dearth of public spirit, and want of virtue" and marveled at the "fertility in all the low arts" when the new officers were being chosen. The only real reinforcement he received while the new army was being formed was Martha's arrival on December 11; the sustenance of her quiet, pleasant presence certainly meant much as her husband wrestled with his apparently insoluble problems. But, by one expedient or another, they were solved, and early in January, while the returns disclosed only 5,582 men present and fit for duty, there were 8,212 enlisted for the new year; although there was a troublesome shortage of muskets and powder remained in short supply, the lines were again manned. Washington could untypically but pardonably boast:

Search the vast volumes of history through, and I much question whether a case similar to ours is to be found; to wit, to maintain a post against the flower of the British troops for six months together, without [powder], and at the end of them to have one army disbanded and another to raise within the same distance of a reinforced enemy.

The remanning of the lines was the only bright spot. From England came news of the king's speech to Parliament in October in which he called for an all-out effort to crush the rebellion. From Canada Washington learned of the failure of Arnold and Montgomery to take Quebec, with the latter's death; the situation there was not lost but it was in grave peril. Obviously the war had turned into a long-term effort. Charles Lee was sent to New York City, a likely English target, to improve its defenses and Washington dropped his resistance to long-term enlistments and bounties, which he had opposed as wasteful.

Washington was beginning to understand and accept some of the peculiarities of a citizen-army; the men needed the bounties to help their families subsist while they were serving, not to profit from the public's necessity. Washington's progress in this area was uneven; he implicitly relied on the standard European military treatises for advice on discipline, but these treatises were based on the aristocratic European armies. They disregarded the motive force of patriotism and the personal stake which all Americans who opposed English policy had in the struggle. However, even a superficial reading of his general orders shows the value he placed on these feelings. In a sense, he operated on two levels as commander-in-chief: when dealing with the Congress, he constantly tried to get them to form a "real" army, i.e., on the model he had observed when serving with Braddock and Forbes; but when he had to work with the daily problems of keeping his army in being, he accommodated himself to the realities of his rag-tag forces and bent his ingenuity to keeping them together as best he could and however he could. Often enough, ingenuity was all he had.[6]

With spring more than 14,000 men were available for duty around Boston and again Washington's thoughts turned to an attack on the city, one which would wipe out the English. And again the council of war restrained him. A quantity of artillery had been brought to

Cambridge from the captured English fort at Ticonderoga; it was decided to emplace the guns on Dorchester Heights, commanding Boston from the south, thus forcing the enemy either to come out against the Americans or to evacuate the city. Because of the cold weather, fortifications could not be dug, but an inventive Massachusetts officer suggested using chandeliers, wooden frames filled with hay and brush, as the basis for a prefabricated fort. After appropriate preparations, the instant citadel was put in place on the night of March 4–5, with no English reaction. A violent storm had prevented any response until the Dorchester lines were so strong that an attack would be suicidal. The English commander, Sir William Howe, had decided for strategic reasons to evacuate the city at the first opportunity. On March 8 Washington was told informally of the impending departure of the enemy, thus confirming his prediction that "they must either give us battle, or quit their present possessions." By the seventeenth the answer was clear; all the troops, what equipment they could not destroy, and about a thousand Loyalists sailed from the city's wharves; the siege of Boston was over.

Although the Congress congratulated their victorious general with a gold medal and Harvard College awarded him the degree Doctor of Laws, *honoris causa,* retrospection tempers the enthusiasm shown at the time. His best efforts had been able only to make the English uncomfortable in Boston; their decision to evacuate had been made before the emplacements on Dorchester had appeared and was the result not of American strategic brilliance but rather of Howe's calm assessment of the assets and liabilities of Boston, chiefly the latter, as a base. Washington had done well to hold the varied—in numbers, training, and equipment—units of his army together and maintain the siege, especially having had, in essence, to replace one army with another. But he was going to have to learn to be more discreet; some of his letters to Lund Washington, managing affairs at Mount Vernon for him, had become public knowledge; they were exceedingly critical, unfairly so, of New England morals and courage. All the general could lamely, but truthfully, say was that he had changed his mind. His impetuosity would have to be reined in by himself rather than by his counselors; further, his desire to mount an attack on Boston was not founded on an accurate understanding of the enemy's strength and disposition and his own army's abilities, but on his eagerness to end the war with a splendid *coup de main.* An experienced gambler, even if he cannot wait until they are favorable, at least calculates the odds. Washington would learn the importance of intelligence the hard way. He also showed his old tendency to do much of his own paperwork; paradoxically, by tying him up with busy work, it decreased his authority over his subordinates when they were sent to distant areas. Soon Charles Lee in New York, and later in South Carolina, as well as Schuyler, were communicating directly with the Congress; thus unity of command was lost and material for future misunderstandings and quarrels was supplied. But this was grist for future mills to grind. For now, the general was amply pleased that "my reputation stands fair, that my conduct hitherto has given universal satisfaction." That "satisfaction" was the only compensation he was asking for his services, and he would not always be paid as generously as he was after Boston. On April 4 he left for New York City, Howe's expected destination.

New York City, then clustered at the southern tip of Manhattan Island, was one of the most important commercial cities in the colonies and was second only to Philadelphia in population. Its island location, combined with the certain ability of the enemy to command the waters around it, made it almost impossible to defend; only the unlikely prospect of blocking the Hudson River could deny the city to the enemy for very long. The Congress ordered Washington to defend the city and, despite the difficulty of the task, it is hard to disagree with them. The psychological implications of abandoning the city without a fight could have been disastrous to the fragile patriot cause although, as events proved, if the cause could survive when the city was actually lost, it could probably survive anything. [7]

Charles Lee had already studied the site and made suggestions, only partially implemented when Washington arrived, for improving the city's defenses. After several weeks on the scene Washington hoped it could be put in a "very respectable posture of defense," although he was concerned about shortages of men and powder. Ironically, at the critical moment, both were plentiful—but defeat still came.

In mid-May, there were only 6,700 men fit for duty in the American camp against an estimated rock-bottom 8,000 needed for its defense. Faced with the continued deterioration of the army in Canada, the Congress told Washington to make do with a draft of 20,000 militia from the northern colonies with half again as many men held in reserve in New Jersey. Despite these official decisions, Washington had only 7,400 fit for duty six weeks later, with a good bit yet to be done on the city's defenses. All this became more than academic when an English fleet entered New York harbor and anchored off Staten Island; by the afternoon of June 29 more than 100 vessels had entered the road. The General reported the event somberly to the Congress and promised "to make the best disposition I can for our troops, in order to give [the enemy] a proper reception, and to prevent the ruin and destruction they are meditating against us." With this he began to clear the field as well as he could.

After tiptoeing around the measure for months, the Congress helped by approving, on July 2, Richard Henry Lee's resolution that "these United Colonies are, and of right ought to be, free and independent States," with Thomas Jefferson's explanation of what had driven George III's hitherto loyal subjects to this ultimate step sent out to the world two days later. Washington was not one of those who needed convincing by Jefferson's ingenious reasoning; since he had assumed command, he had often acted as if the colonies were already independent and, by so doing, he helped to bring about the Congress's decision. In January he had approved "the sound doctrine and unanswerable reasoning" of Tom Paine's argument for the necessity of America's independence which the English-born pamphleteer had put forward in *Common Sense*. In April Washington had dropped the distinction he had previously maintained of always calling the enemy the "ministerial army," not the royal army; now he thought the distinction "idle," thus anticipating the Congress's decision by three months. As he had in the past and would again in the future, he had let himself slide into a basic decision by letting events mount up until there was only one way to go; when he sent a copy of the Declaration to the Massachusetts assembly, he noted that it was "Impelled by Necessity and a Repetition of Injuries insufferable, without the most distant prospect of relief"; in short, there was nothing else to do. The Congress had taken a few months longer to get to that point than had its general.

But then the necessity of the case was much more obvious to the general, facing, as he did, more than 20,000 enemy troops, including a number of German mercenaries, hired from their princes under terms suggesting the rental of horses, not men. They were dubbed Hessians, after one of the larger contingents from Hesse-Cassel. General Sir William Howe, coming down from Halifax, where he had reorganized the troops he had taken from Boston, was in command. He was very much the model of an eighteenth-century general, proceeding slowly and with great care, always maneuvering his force so as to gain the maximum advantage before the guns spoke, then securing a victory with the smallest possible loss of his expensive soldiers. That these tactics would not yield the destruction of the American army was probably agreeable to Howe, who hoped to end the rebellion by convincing the Americans that resistance was hopeless; after that, reconciliation would only be hindered by memories of bloody battles. After offering the king's pardon and having it spurned by an indignant Washington, who protested that the Americans had done nothing of which they had to be pardoned, Howe began to move his army to Long Island. The Americans had anticipated this and placed themselves on a naturally strong height, just across the East River from the city. Their height was pierced by four roads, three of which were adequately guarded. Unfortunately the fourth, patrolled by only a small militia force, was the one Howe's main force took. On the morning of August 27, while the English annoyed the American lines from the front, Howe neatly outflanked them by moving over the Jamaica Road, at the extreme left of the rebel lines. The Battle of Long Island was over almost before it began and the Americans lost two brigadier-generals, James Sullivan and William Alexander (who claimed a Scottish peerage and insisted on the title Lord Stirling), and about 1,400 other officers and men; the English loss was less than 400. Inadequate reconnaissance, an uncertain command situation, and too few men defending too long a line were certainly mitigating factors in the American defeat, but the fact remains that Washington had made a very poor disposition of his resources and his men had suffered for it.[8]

The Americans retreated to earthen fortifications on Brooklyn Heights and faced twice their number of enemy troops, with the East River blocking any further retreat. Howe shunned the cost of a frontal attack and began a slow but man-saving siege; further, if the navy could come up the East River, the Americans would have no place to go but to English prison camps. An American council of war on August 29 reached the only possible decision: evacuate the men immediately. An unusual late summer northeaster came to the rescue and held the enemy ships back with its contrary winds. A motley collection of small boats manned by Colonel John Glover's regiment of Marblehead, Massachusetts, fishermen took all the men and their equipment off during the night of August 29–30. The force had been saved, but to what purpose? It was very like the famous move from the frying pan into the fire. Now Washington's force was concentrated on Manhattan Island, which had only one bridge to the mainland—Kingsbridge, at the island's northern tip—and an uncharacteristically quick move by Howe could gather it in before

Glover's men could work another minor miracle. And the Congress denied Washington's request for permission to burn the city to deny its buildings to the enemy. Even if it were captured, they counted on its quick recovery.

Thus Washington was apparently committed to the defense of an indefensible city with an army in which he no longer had any confidence; "I had no doubt in my mind of defending this place . . . if the men would do their duty, but this I despair of." Desertion from the militia became commonplace and began to infect the men enlisted for the year. Even before September 14, when permission arrived from the Congress, Washington had begun to evacuate the island; the process was interrupted by an English landing from the East River on the fifteenth. The untrained, ill-equipped militia at the landing site broke and ran, an example which the other troops in the area unfortunately followed; Washington, riding to the scene from his headquarters, rallied some soldiers into making a stand but, as soon as the English appeared, they resumed their panicky, disorderly flight, causing Washington to despair: "Good God! Have I got such troops as these?" as he sat his horse, almost waiting for the oncoming enemy to capture him. Collecting himself, he ordered a defensive line secured along Harlem Heights, hilly ground to the north of a valley running northeastward across the island, with what troops remained under some discipline. General Putnam, acting on his own, had already gotten the men in the city, south of the English landing place, moving north along the west side of the island; practically all of them escaped before the English had thrown their line across to the Hudson, but large quantities of materiel were lost. Thus Washington still had most of his army, but the day had seemed to confirm his earlier fears that they would not fight.

A small encounter the next day between American and English scouting parties south of the Heights led to a larger action in which the Continentals gave the redcoats as good as they were getting and showed that they could fight, and fight well. The Battle of Harlem Heights "inspirited our troops prodigiously" but their commander needed more convincing evidence before he could be "inspirited." For the moment he was doubting even himself and he poured out his hurt and confusion to cousin Lund; he did not know what to do, could see no good coming of his continued service, yet he was assured that he would irreparably harm the Cause by resigning; he could gain neither fame nor success under the present system of recruiting and had neither comfort nor peace—"I never was in such an unhappy, divided state since I was born." Then the torrent of feeling eased, and characteristically but anticlimactically he concluded by cautioning Lund not to show the letter to anyone else. The task was his, and he would stay with it to the end, whenever that was.

The army lingered at the Heights for almost a month until Howe jolted Washington out of his despairing lethargy with an attempt to land on the mainland above Kingsbridge; everyone except the men manning Fort Washington, one of a pair of forts meant to deny the Hudson to the English, was immediately removed from the island. Once off Manhattan, Washington had to move to the high ground north of the Croton River or he might be pinned against the Hudson; before he could get there, he and Howe met on October 28 in the inconclusive Battle of White Plains. The encounter was a success for the Americans in that the men fought well and it gave them enough time to beat a safe retreat to the heights above the Croton; it also suited their commander's desire to avoid a major battle "or put anything to the risk, unless compelled by a necessity into which we ought never to be drawn." Now, although the army was in a naturally strong position, desertion and supply problems continued and the Congress had again delayed enlistment plans for the next year's army; soon Washington would be in the same position he had been in at Cambridge, but this year the situation was much more fluid; everything could very easily be lost. Battered by two months of almost unrelieved defeat and retreat, Washington followed the advice of a council and did what he had always strenuously resisted, divide his army. He left 3,000 men with Major-General William Heath to guard the supply route from New England; 7,000 remained temporarily with Charles Lee (back from a successful defense of Charleston, S.C.), while Washington took 2,000 with him into New Jersey, where he expected to find a reserve of 5,000 militia. The Congress had, the summer before, planned a "Flying Camp" of militia forces to be used as the commander-in-chief felt necessary; congressional resolutions were one thing and their execution quite another, and the camp had never been formed, but no one had told Washington. On November 13, all he found at Fort Lee, the New Jersey twin to Fort Washington, were 2,700 men under the command of Major-General Nathanael Greene.

An armchair general can easily see that Fort Washington was a poorly designed fort in an impossible location, but armchair generals have quiet and time, both missing completely from the life of the harried and bewildered commander of the American forces. Greene was left in charge of both forts while Washington puzzled out his next move. Suddenly a massive enemy attack was hurled against Fort Washington on the sixteenth, and the post's defects became obvious. Within hours the post's commander, Colonel Robert Magaw, had no recourse but to surrender the almost 2,800 men and a large store of materiel which Greene had left there. A few days later Washington blamed the Congress for wanting the river blocked and Greene for reinforcing the fort only days before its fall; but the fairest assessment of the incident he ever made came three years later when he admitted "that warfare in my mind, and hesitation" had helped bring about the loss. Despite Greene's command, Washington had three days on the scene where he should have done something about the risky situation across the Hudson: the responsibility was his.[9]

Washington began to plan moving his slightly more than 2,000 men down toward another American force on the Raritan River when Howe, moving uncharacteristically fast, moved a force across the Hudson early on the twentieth and moved south, hoping to catch the Americans at Fort Lee. Local tradition has it that a plowman, working early, saw the redcoats and rode ahead to warn the garrison. Taking only their powder and shot, the Continentals got away just in time, clearing a critical crossroads, the Liberty Pole in the English Neighborhood (now Englewood), just as the English advance party came in sight. Except for the few shots exchanged there, the Americans got away unscathed. Crossing the Hackensack River on the "New Bridge," the Americans reached a haven for the night, but, pinned between the Hackensack and Passaic Rivers, in flat country with no natural defenses, Washington had to keep his small force moving south. For the next two weeks, with only a few days' rest, the men slogged through the mud in a cold November rain until they had passed through New Jersey and put the Delaware behind them.

Washington now tried to concentrate his forces again and ordered Charles Lee to bring his units to the Delaware; but that worthy, impressed with his success in the South and Washington's manifest mistakes in the New York campaign, procrastinated and presumed to deal with his commander as an equal. Further, Washington discovered, inadvertently, that Joseph Reed, his aide, was secretly corresponding with Lee about the commander's indecision and lack of strategic sense. Washington, who felt he needed both men, swallowed his pride and let the incident pass. The success or failure of the war was more important than his own feelings. And Lee was soon removed by his own folly from the action; sleeping, for comfort's sake, too far from his men, he was captured by an English patrol on December 13. This freed Sullivan, his second-in-command, recently exchanged, to bring on his force of 2,000 men to the main army, clustered on the far side of the Delaware above Trenton. All the boats had been taken by the Americans so Howe settled his men down along the river below Trenton and back up the road to New Brunswick and began to collect loyalty oaths from repentant New Jersey patriots.[10]

Despite his settled appearance, Washington was convinced that Howe would move on Philadelphia as soon as the river froze, giving him an easy passage across it. And the enlistments of most of Washington's men would expire with the year; of the 8,000 he could concentrate along the Delaware, only 1,400 to 1,500 would be left on January 1, 1777. He had to blunt or stop the English advance and gain time to gather a new army. Faced with such desperate circumstances, paradoxically, the only hope was to resume the offensive and throw the enemy off stride, perhaps long enough to discourage any more fighting that winter. As early as December 14, Washington had thought of attacking the Hessian units across the Delaware in Trenton and Bordentown. Complicated plans for a three-pronged advance were made; Pennsylvania militia would strike at Bordentown while a second force would strike at Trenton from the south; this was to coincide with an attack by Washington's force from the north. Christmas night, masked by a snow and sleet storm, Washington moved his 2,400 men, supported by eighteen cannon (much more than usual, but he knew his men needed all the help they could get), across the icy river. Before the men separated into two columns, Washington moved among them, solemnly urging them to stay near their officers. For once a divided American force kept well synchronized and both columns went into action at the same time. Neither of the other units crossed the river, so 400 of the Hessian garrison escaped to the south before the town was surrounded. Two hours of close-quarter fighting brought the surrender of the rest of the garrison at the cost of only four American wounded. More than 100 Hessians were killed or wounded, and 1,000 were captured. Surveying his situation, Washington decided to recross the river immediately. Alone, his own men tired and chilled to the bone, with prisoners to handle, there was little more he could do, for the moment, in New Jersey.

Washington's brief but circumstantial account of the victory noted the spirited behavior of the men; when it "came to the charge, each seemed to vie with the other in pressing forward" and no unit could be singled out without doing injustice to the others. If Trenton did anything, it helped to cure the lack of confidence Washington had had in his own men since Manhattan. But, of course, it did much more than that. More of a raid than a battle, its military significance was not great; but, psychologically, Trenton came at exactly the right moment to enspirit the Americans, who believed that all was about to be lost, and to discourage the English, whose easy progress through New Jersey had them believing all was about to be won. Now both sides quickly recast their plans for the immediate future. Howe called back one of his more active subordinates, Lord Cornwallis, as he was ready to embark for England and sent him down to Princeton, eleven miles from Trenton, with reinforcements while the Hessian units were pulled back from the Delaware. Washington, without the luxury of reserves to call in, had rather more difficult decisions to make.

Before he could do anything, Washington had to ensure that he would have an army after the first of the year. Without knowing that the Congress had granted him dictatorial powers for six months, he offered his Continental regiments a $10.00 bounty for an additional month's service. Responding to his description of the next few weeks as "the crisis which is to decide our destiny" and saying that "we know not how to spare you," enough signed to furnish a hard core of Continentals to bolster the Pennsylvania and New Jersey militia coming out for two month's service.

A move across the Delaware could appear to be an advance but still leave several escape routes should the numerically superior enemy be encountered unfavorably. On the first day of 1777, Washington's men joined Pennsylvania militia at Trenton. Early on the second, a strong American scouting party encountered Cornwallis, advancing from Princeton; for the rest of the day, they fought a stiff delaying action, permitting Washington to arrange his army behind the Assunpink Creek. By afternoon the two forces faced each other across the rivulet, spanned by a narrow stone bridge; Cornwallis decided he had the "old fox" bagged between the creek and river and would wait for the next day to claim his trophy. Leaving behind some men to keep the fires lit and to make noise, so Cornwallis could sleep undisturbed, the Americans marched south and then looped around to the north to strike at enemy units left behind in Princeton and perhaps continue on to New Brunswick, where a £70,000 war chest and large quantities of matériel had been left.

The ruse worked. American forward units encountered a surprised

English officer bringing his men forward to Cornwallis, on the outskirts of Princeton early on the morning of the third. Despite an early reverse, and the death of Brigadier-General Hugh Mercer, the Americans rallied, under the personal direction of Washington, and forced the English to break and run. Other enemy units were pinned down and forced to surrender, including 194 in the College of New Jersey's Nassau Hall, where one well-placed cannon shot, according to tradition, decapitated a portrait of George II inside the front door of the hall and ended its use as a redoubt. The shot was fired by Colonel Alexander Hamilton's New York artillery; his competent work soon placed him on Washington's staff, where he would stay until 1781.

Assessing the situation in a hurried conference held without even dismounting, Washington and his generals decided the men were too fatigued to continue on to New Brunswick, especially when the relatively fresh Cornwallis troops would soon be close on their heels. Destroying a bridge to slow down the English, the Americans put some distance between themselves and the enemy before resting and then moving to winter quarters in Morristown, safely beyond the Ramapo Mountains in northern New Jersey. With Washington on his flank, Howe moved all his men back, leaving only garrisons at New Brunswick and Perth Amboy; New Jersey was, to all intents and purposes, again a patriot state.

To say that the 1776 campaign had educated Washington is to restate the obvious; any general is constantly learning—and relearning—the lessons of war. But Washington needed a good bit more of this than most of the generals he faced, and he obtained it in the same school they attended, that of experience. His mistakes during the fighting in and around New York City were many and obvious, but they were mitigated by the military unsuitability of a city for which it was psychologically necessary that a fight be made; he certainly could have done better, but the decision to fight for the city was correct. Throughout the campaign, the lack of competent officers threw too much of the burden on the commander-in-chief, who also had to contend with disloyalty and carping criticism; this was a factor in the fatigue and indecision shown at various times. Washington's loss of confidence in his men must also have hindered him from trying to make a stand instead of retreating. But he had also begun to learn the assets, as well as the liabilities, of the American soldier, especially the short-term usefulness of the militia when bolstered, as they had been at Princeton, by seasoned Continentals. The fine performance of the troops was, as it must always be, one of the chief ingredients in the American victories of December 26 and January 3; in the words of one of Washington's favorite plays, Addison's *Cato,* the soldiers not only attained success, they deserved it. And so did their commander. Against the ponderous, slow-moving caution of Howe, Washington had been able to snatch, if not victory, at least survival from the jaws of defeat. The weariness and indecision which had marked him fell away as he made and remade plans as the necessity of the moment required and as he took intelligent risks, not careless risks such as at Fort Washington. However, as successful as Trenton and Princeton were, they do not make Washington one of the great captains of history; the contribution he made to the American victory was in the quality of his leadership. As has already been seen, he was often discouraged, and his letters to his family read like a catalogue of prospective horrors—"the game is nearly up" was one of his favorite clichés—but he never gave up and associates remarked how his command improved during times of acute stress. During the last four months of 1776 Washington experienced enough frustration and defeat to justify a resignation, but he instead extended himself and his men and brought about a spectacular turn of fortune. Trenton and Princeton are perhaps most important as examples of the commander-in-chief's refusal to accept defeat.

The army spent an uncomfortable winter at Morristown, plagued by both food shortages and disease. The core of less than 1,000 Continentals were supplemented by New Jersey militia who spent their brief tours of duty harassing the English garrisons in New Brunswick and Perth Amboy. Washington kept the size of his small force such a closely guarded secret that even some congressmen complained of keeping "hordes" of men in idleness. But that same Congress grandly resolved to raise an army of 75,000; as before, the Congress's willingness to resolve was one thing, its ability to deliver quite another. Eventually 8,000 men enlisted under its resolution arrived at Morristown.

Moving out of winter quarters in May, Washington placed his army just above New Brunswick and, through June, refused Howe's invitation to move down onto the coastal plain which began below New Brunswick. Unwilling to advance toward Philadelphia with the Continentals on his flank, Howe called the dance off early in July and left New Jersey. Realizing that the cause could be "advanced otherwise than by fighting," especially if the fighting might lose him his army, Washington had bought precious time with his defensive maneuvering and demonstrated a lot more patience and self-control than the Colonel of the Virginia Regiment had ever demonstrated.

Now it was Washington's turn to be confused by Howe. Knowing of the English thrust down Lake Champlain under Brigadier-General John Burgoyne, he was uncertain whether Howe would take ship and move up the Hudson toward Burgoyne or down the Bay and sail around New Jersey to hit Philadelphia. Marching and counter-marching through central Jersey while Howe sent out puzzling signals broke down the already shaky American supply system. Washington did not need it but the uncertainty regarding Howe's destination was a fine demonstration of the mobility the Royal Navy gave the English. On August 22, Washington learned that Howe's fleet was moving up Chesapeake Bay. He had been scared away from the Delaware River by exaggerated reports of its navigational hazards and the American defenses and now was going to strike at Philadelphia from the south. Making a virtue of necessity, Washington had the army cleaned up, a fresh sprig of green placed in every man's hat, and marched them through the city as they moved to fend off Howe. Although admiring, Massachusetts Congressman John Adams had to note: "Our soldiers have not yet quite the air of soldiers," but their general had learned that spirit could make up for cosmetic deficiencies.

In some respects, Philadelphia presented the same dilemma New York had; militarily of no great significance, it still could not be abandoned without a fight. As the seat of the Congress, it was the closest thing to a capital the young republic had and it was also an important commercial and manufacturing center. There the resemblance ended; although on a peninsula between two rivers, there was no great advantage for English sea power as the rivers were shallow and hard to navigate; otherwise the city's approaches were over flat or rolling terrain. Along the route of Howe's advance from the south the closest thing to a natural barrier was the Brandywine Creek; deep enough to be crossed only at several fords, it entered the Delaware at Wilmington. Facing an army of 18,000, Washington arranged his force of 11,000 along the creek's banks on September 10 and awaited the enemy. Early the next morning, in a hazy dawn that promised a repeat of the stifling heat of the last few days, the American center was attacked; the line was held but contradictory intelligence reports from the American right, commanded by Sullivan, confused Washington and he halted an attack on the enemy center and went himself to investigate. He found Sullivan under a heavy attack, caught while changing position to meet the enemy; all he could do was help the badly mauled Americans disengage. The intelligence reports were accurate; it was Washington's poor knowledge of the terrain which made them seem contradictory; and when the crisis came, his response was slow, for much of the day he acted "as if he had been in a daze." Yet, for all the commander's shortcomings, the day was not a complete disaster. Although the Americans suffered twice as many casualties as the enemy, they remained on the field until ordered to leave and then left in good order, although they later got hopelessly mixed up. Further, the defeat seemed to discourage few; the feeling among the men seemed to be that the next encounter might be a victory. And an English review of the year's operations concurred: "the rebels were not disheartened; and Mr. Washington exerted himself with ability and diligence to repair his defeat."[11]

The men re-formed and some additional units were brought in from the Hudson. Washington maneuvered his ill-fed, ill-clad (more than 1,000 were barefoot) men, trying to parry Howe's thrusts toward Philadelphia. In the confused maneuvering that followed, Howe feinted toward Reading, where a large American supply store was located, pulling Washington well away from the city, then the English general neatly countermarched and entered the capital on September 23. Now the unimportance of the city became obvious to everyone. The Congress had long since fled and all important supplies had been removed; only the shell of a city with its Loyalist sympathizers was left for the enemy. Further, it remained to be seen if Howe could hold the city. American forts, erected to guard obstructions in the narrow Delaware channel, were putting up a stiff resistance; if Howe could not be supplied by the navy, he might have to give up the city. The river forts, almost unsupported, held out until mid-November, by which time Washington had shown the English he was far from beaten.

Howe had placed the main portion of his army at Germantown, about fifteen miles northwest of the city, where their detached location almost seemed to invite an American attack. With the available men, Washington contrived an elaborate four-pronged pincers movement whose strength was concentrated in the center. Although hindered by poorly drawn orders, the attack began auspiciously early on October 4, and the Americans drove the enemy back almost into the main camp. Then things began to fall apart. A quick-rising fog confused the advancing Continentals, some of whom fired on each other; ammunition ran short just as fresh English units were encountered; and a precipitate retreat left Nathanael Greene's column alone. Militia units, the outside pincers, were either beaten back or else never reached the scene. Although the American retreat was disorderly, a rear guard was organized and kept the English at a distance.

Analyses of Germantown often focus on the complexity of the battle plan as the reason for defeat, but the fog, the confused firing on each other, and the shortage of ammunition were at least equally responsible. It is not often enough remembered that the Americans almost won the battle, complicated orders and green officers to the contrary notwithstanding. And, as with Brandywine, solace could be found in defeat; the Americans fought well and, as Washington reported to the Congress, "the day was rather unfortunate than injurious." Further, news of the battle, reported none too accurately in France, combined with news of the surrender of a large English army to Major-General Horatio Gates at Saratoga in mid-October to create such a favorable impression at the French court that an alliance was signed in February 1778.[12]

A month of apparently aimless maneuvering north and west of Philadelphia followed until Washington settled the men down at Valley Forge, eighteen miles up the Schuylkill River from Philadelphia. He had wanted to take them into the interior near the Congress, which was now safely ensconced at York, 100 miles to the west, or else down to Wilmington, but strong protests from Pennsylvania kept him in the Philadelphia area. He obeyed the civilian authorities although, as he noted almost sarcastically, it was easy enough to draw up remonstrances when warm and well fed, much easier than seeing to it that Pennsylvania contributed her share to the army's supplies. The area selected for the camp had been drained dry of supplies, and "wintering in this desert," as the foreign volunteer, Johann deKalb described it, would be difficult enough for an army with an effective supply organization. Now, in addition to the perennial problem of recruiting a new army and the constant problems of indiscipline and poor officers, Washington would have to be his own supply officer.

Valley Forge has become a symbol of the trials which the Continental Army underwent because of the too-often ineffectual support which the Congress gave it, and it is difficult to exaggerate the privations which the men endured. Entering the camp in poor condition because of their inadequate clothing and constant marching, the only lack they were able to correct themselves was shelter; by building rough log huts, at least a measure of comfort was secured.

But there were rarely enough foodstuffs on hand for Washington to relax; the slightest interruption to the flow of supplies and the men were reduced to meager allotments of flour or corn meal, with sometimes nothing at all. Local foraging was fruitless, and before the winter was over the net had been cast as far as North Carolina to bring food to the men. The commissariat had recently been reformed and the men administering it were inexperienced or incompetent; hence much of Washington's time was taken up with begging letters to state authorities, obtaining food wherever he could. The overwork caused by this constant problem may have helped bring on the irritability he displayed during the episode known as the Conway Cabal.[13]

The Cabal took its name from Brigadier-General Thomas Conway, an Irish-born French officer, one of the many French officers who came over both recommended and unrecommended, expecting to show the ignorant Americans the finer points of the art of war. Conway had demonstrated his competence at the Brandywine and Germantown and was angling for promotion to major-general over the heads of several senior American officers. The Congress did promote him and made him Inspector-General, attached to the Board of War, a group of full-time administrators, taking the place of congressional committees, who would try to satisfy the needs of the army. Washington objected to the promotion because of the injury it did to the American brigadiers, and Congress delayed it. But the commander-in-chief became suspicious when he learned that Conway was corresponding with Horatio Gates, whose success at Saratoga contrasted strikingly with the Philadelphia campaign's failures. The former quartermaster-general, Thomas Mifflin, was also connected with Conway when he and Gates were appointed to the board. It is doubtful that these three did anything more than exchange letters critical of Washington's conduct of the war. Nor was there widespread discontent with their general among the Congress although some recognized that there was danger in the idolization of any military figure, even one as principled as Washington; John Adams rejoiced at Saratoga, not only for its military benefits but also because it permitted "a certain citizen to be wise, virtuous, and good, without thinking him a deity or a saviour." More to the point, Elbridge Gerry complained that the extreme reaction from Washington's officers, especially of his staff to the Conway promotion, was hindering the Congress in its constitutional prerogative of selecting officers. For his part, Washington seemed convinced that there was indeed a plot to see Gates "exalted on the ruin of my reputation and influence." His anxiety on this score was compounded of several ingredients: the overwork mentioned previously, his sensitivity to criticism, and his regard for his public standing. Even as the Colonel of the Virginia Regiment, Washington had not received criticism well; now, although he often claimed he was willing to accept informed criticism, civilian comment was usually rejected as uninformed, and now military comment was a symptom of a plot. His concern about his reputation was more understandable; he was serving for the one coin he regarded above all others, the good opinion of his fellow citizens, and anything which menaced this would always provoke a strong reaction from him. The furor began to die down when Conway, seeing the untenability of his position, resigned in January 1778; with this marplot removed from the scene, Washington recovered his composure as he continued to wrestle with the never-ending problems of keeping the army together and planning for the new campaign.[14]

Despite the trials of the winter camp at Valley Forge, one clear gain was made. Late in February Friedrich von Steuben presented himself at Washington's headquarters with a freshly signed commission. Although his background and experience had been embellished, his ability was real and he quickly devised a common and simplified system of drill and maneuver to replace the different ones used in the army. His work was soon rewarded with appointment as inspector-general and promotion to major-general. Although it is possible to overestimate the work he did at Valley Forge—after all, he did not find an untrained mob there—the army that marched in pursuit of the enemy in the spring of 1778 was a more dependable force, and Steuben contributed materially to that improvement.[15]

Nor was that the only improvement that came to the cause during the otherwise grim winter of 1777–78. The Americans no longer stood alone; in February, convinced the rebels were capable of sustaining their effort against the English, the French had signed treaties of commerce and alliance with the Congress's representatives. Washington's reaction was typically both hopeful and cautious: "Calmness and serenity, seems likely to succeed in some measure, those dark and tempestuous clouds which at times appeared ready to overwhelm us. The game, whether well or ill played hitherto, seems now to be verging fast to a favorable issue." Now care would have to be taken that the Americans did not relax and let their new allies take over. And there was very little to relax over. As usual, with the spring already half-gone, the supply system was in disarray and only a little more than one-half of the 20,000 troops authorized for the year were in camp. These would have to deal with the 10,000 English troops in Philadelphia and an additional 6,000 divided between New York and Newport. As ever, militia would have to supplement the regulars.

As the American generals were deliberating themselves into inaction, the new English commander, Lieutenant-General Sir Henry Clinton, took the initiative and began to move his army across New Jersey, evacuating Philadelphia. Prepared to move, the Americans followed close behind as the English crossed the Delaware on June 17. Since Clinton had had to take most of his baggage in a train of 1,500 wagons, Washington scented the possibility of striking a substantial blow at the long, straggling English columns, a possibility his generals were seriously divided over. Because of seniority, Charles Lee (recently exchanged for an English general), strenuously opposed to a major attack, commanded the advance guard with vague orders "to act as occasion may serve."

The occasion came, in sultry heat which reached near 100°, on June 28, at Monmouth Courthouse, southeast of New Brunswick. Fighting with his back against a field scarred by three morasses, the only way back a narrow causeway, Lee soon became convinced he had struck the main body, not the rear guard of the enemy, and ordered a retreat. As Washington came to the battle, a confused withdrawal had already begun. He brusquely asked Lee why he was retreating, to which Lee stammered something about poor intelligence. Turning from Lee, Washington organized a temporary line and then brought the main body of his troops into a strong defensive position in back of the morasses and there the two armies fought it out to a stalemate. The Americans, expecting to renew the battle the next day, slept on their arms, but the morning light revealed that Clinton had quietly pulled out during the night. The Americans faced an empty field.[16]

Disappointed at the indecisive results—even the casualties were roughly equal, about 360 on each side—Washington did not claim a victory in his report to the Congress, nor did he mention Lee's conduct. But there was an item for the credit side; the men had fought well, especially in their maneuvering under fire. Steuben's drilling was already paying dividends. Now the strangest sequel of the battle occurred. Lee asked his commander, in an insulting fashion, for an explanation of his conduct on the day of the battle. Clearly looking for a confrontation, Lee was soon obliged by being charged with disobeying orders by not attacking, making an *"unnecessary, disorderly, and shameful retreat,"* and disrespect to his general. The resulting court-martial settled nothing, as the testimony on the accused's conduct was confused and contradictory. Nevertheless Lee was found guilty and suspended from command for a year, a mild punishment which did not fit the seriousness of the first two charges. And this was as it should be. The real point of the situation was in the third charge. Lee, ever confident of his own superior ability and contemptuous of Washington's conduct of his command, had challenged the commander-in-chief directly. The court-martial was really asked to choose between Washington or Lee, between the symbol of American resistance to England and an Englishman whose attachment to the cause was suspected by many. The Congress confirmed the verdict and Lee never resumed his command. Ironically, Washington's fault was the greater at Monmouth; he had permitted a man who openly doubted the ability of the Americans to stand up to the English to command when he very much wanted a vigorous attack to be made. But the army and the Congress were not considering the merits of generals, but rather of leaders, and there Washington was clearly the superior.

The unpleasant memories of the near-thing at Monmouth and the Lee court-martial probably passed quickly away when Washington learned of the arrival of a French fleet off Sandy Hook; his first thought was to enlist it in an attempt against the English garrison in New York City. But this had to be set aside when the French ships-of-the-line could not get over the bar at the mouth of the harbor. They did help in an attack on Newport Island which began well and then ended abruptly, unsuccessfully, and acrimoniously when the fleet withdrew and left John Sullivan and an American force almost stranded on the island. The Americans were gotten off safely but Sullivan let the French know what he thought of them, and the alliance was off on an uneasy course.

Thus the campaigning season of 1778 ended with little more accomplished than the recovery of Philadelphia, certainly not brought about by American arms, and the first, inglorious attempt to cooperate with the French. With the men comfortably placed in winter quarters, Washington rode to Philadelphia to confer with the Congress about the next campaign. The stay produced little more than frustration for the general. He viewed with dismay the high living and apparent unconcern of congressmen and others about the deficiencies of the army and the fast-falling value of Continental currency. All this he lamented, but quietly and privately to friends in Virginia whom he urged to cooperate in sending the best Virginians to the Congress so that at least one state would do its part. As he doubtless realized later, he was living through what was probably the war's lowest point, when the Americans seemed incapable of helping themselves and the French of offering nothing save vague promises. Spring saw the same old story: too few men, too few supplies—always scarcity where plenty was needed, apparently because few civilians could or would match the dedication of the soldiers and their dispirited commander. The constant toil of fighting a war on the cheap was telling on Washington. In April 1779 he complained that it was "a melancholy thing to see such a decay of public virtue, and the fairest prospects overcast and clouded by a host of infamous harpies who, to acquire a little pelf, would involve this great continent in inextricable ruin." Although he was overstating things, as he usually did when he vented the deep pessimism lying just below his calm exterior, it is also important to note that he never showed the least disposition to take matters into his own hands and, with the army, give law to the Congress which had allowed, if it had not caused, such a situation. If the new republic was generally fortunate in its servants, it was thrice blessed with a commander who could, despite such discouragements, continue to serve loyally and without public complaint.

The year 1779 saw almost as little for Washington's army as 1778 had. Except for some minor actions in the lower Hudson Valley and a successful campaign by Sullivan against the Iroquois, the focus of action had shifted to the South, where first Horatio Gates failed to stop the English, who had already taken Charleston, then Nathanael Greene parried with the enemy in an exhausting campaign that covered most of the Carolinas before it was finished. Perhaps realizing that the Congress's war chest could not support an extensive effort, Washington did not push strongly for more than a holding action in the North. And that is all he got.

The frustration of the summer of 1779 was followed by one of the most difficult winters the Continental Army ever faced. Encamped in the woods near Morristown, New Jersey, the men were ill-served by a supply system which was often ineffectual in good weather, but which broke down completely under the pressure of heavy snows and low temperatures. Washington was forced to condone a requisition on the countryside, always considered the last resort, as he realized that one of the special strengths of the American cause had to be the favor of the country people or all indeed was lost. By this and other expedients the army was again pulled through and prepared, as well as it could be, for the summer's campaigning. If Washington had been willing to let 1779 slip by without a strong American effort, he was not going to let 1780 by. If the French were not convinced that the Americans were serious, he feared they might let the alliance slip into ineffectuality. A special urgency was given to this when the Marquis de Lafayette, a young French volunteer who had originally joined the Americans in 1777 just before Brandywine and had since endeared himself to Washington by his blend of youthful enthusiasm and competence, returned from France with the news that a large French army would presently arrive. Now, if the Americans could match their ally's numbers, perhaps an attack on New York City could be made.

Most of the summer of 1780 was spent waiting for the French army which, when it arrived, proved smaller than expected. Washington's first conference with its commander, Comte de Rochambeau, in September was polite but vague: "We could only combine possible plans on the supposition of possible events and engage mutually to do everything in our powers against the next campaign," the American general recalled later. One clear gain did come from the meeting, however; Washington realized that his nominal command of the combined forces was "upon a very limited scale." If the French general was going to cooperate, it would only be on something he felt bound to succeed.

One step ahead, two steps backward. As he rode back to his headquarters in Tappan, New York, from his talks with the French general, Washington decided to inspect the progress of the fortifications at West Point over which he had recently placed Benedict Arnold, slowly recuperating from a wound suffered at Saratoga. There he found the works in disarray and the post's commander absent. Within a few hours he had learned the reason for both of these strange occurrences. Arnold had been in a treasonous correspondence with the English designed to bring about the handing over of the vital post to the enemy. The plot had been uncovered by the accidental capture of an English officer sent behind the American lines to confer with Arnold, who, informed of the capture by an unsuspecting officer, had fled to the safety of an English vessel. Although the event was one of the more spectacular of the war, it actually had few significant consequences except for those immediately involved. Washington could have been affected if anyone had cared to comment on his placing Arnold in such a vital post, but no one did. He put the best face he could on the incident by commenting to Rochambeau that the remarkable thing was not that there was a traitor—that was only to be expected—but that there had been so few.[17]

Washington should have kept the good spirits he expressed to Rochambeau; he would need them to get through the coming winter. His confused outlook was expressed in a kind of summing up:

> I see nothing before us but accumulating distress. We have been half our time without provision and are like to continue so. We have no Magazines [of munitions], nor money to form them, and in a little time we shall have no Men, if we had money to pay them. We have lived upon expedients till we can live no longer. In a word, the history of the War is a history of false hopes and temporary devices, instead of system and economy. It is in vain, however, to look back, nor is it our business to do so. Our case is not desperate, if virtue exists in the people and there is wisdom among our rulers.

Virtue and wisdom, just the qualities Washington had seen so conspicuously lacking in Philadelphia.

Patience and discretion were also needed, for 1781 brought one of the most terrifying developments any general faced: mutiny. Anthony Wayne's Pennsylvania Line Regiment, quartered near Morristown, had enlisted for three years or the duration. Disgusted with their conditions of service, the men decided their enlistments were for three years only and, under the direction of a committee of sergeants, marched toward Philadelphia. Before Washington could react to the emergency, the Pennsylvania authorities entered the situation and negotiated a settlement favorable to the men. Although Washington feared it might "not only subvert the Pennsylvania Line but have a very pernicious influence on the whole Army," there was nothing he could do but wait for the next incident. Before the end of January, it came. A New Jersey unit, encamped at Pompton, New Jersey, decided to extort its back pay from the state authorities. The officers had talked the men back into their quarters before a picked unit of 500 men under Major-General Robert Howe arrived. On Washington's orders, "a few of the most active and incendiary leaders" were executed and the men returned to their duties. The example he had wanted to give to the army had been given, but Washington did not delude himself. Further mutinies could only be prevented "by rendering the situation of the soldiery more tolerable than it has heretofore been." Patriotism only went so far; good food and warm clothing were also needed.[18]

Washington was also feeling mutinous, but he vented his feelings by a few uncharacteristic displays of ill temper. In February, Alexander Hamilton resigned in a huff from Washington's staff because the general had brusquely rebuked him for a tardy response to a summons; there was fault on both sides, but the initial harshness was the older man's. The following month, after an ineffective and belated attempt by a small French fleet to land some men in the Chesapeake area to relieve the heavy pressure on Greene in North Carolina, Washington vented his anger in an imprudent letter to cousin Lund. As in 1775, the letter fell into English hands and was published. Rochambeau diplomatically hinted that the letter was a forgery, but the American commander refused to take the hint and bluntly stated that, since the letter was private, it should not be noticed. Fortunately for the future of the alliance, Rochambeau decided not to take offense and the affair ended there. [19]

With the failure of the French attempt to land troops in the Chesapeake, Washington was free to argue that an old dream of his, an attack on New York City, would be the most effectual means of relieving the pressure on Greene by possibly inducing the English to pull men north. A Franco-American conference in May resulted in plans for just such an attack. The next month Rochambeau moved his units south from Connecticut and on July 2 the attempt was made. For a variety of reasons, most of them stemming from the natural superiority of the area for an enemy who commanded the waterways around Manhattan, it failed. With this failure, Rochambeau was now free to push a favorite plan of his, moving the whole army to the Chesapeake area. A specific objective presented itself when the English commander in the South, Lord Cornwallis, concentrated his forces on a peninsula between the York and James Rivers, a safe situation as long as the Royal Navy retained its command of the sea. Cornwallis at Yorktown furnished the frame for the puzzle that Washington and Rochambeau would now have to solve; the major pieces that had to be fitted in were the allied armies concentrated around New York City, additional men and provisions, a small French fleet at Newport with the heavy artillery needed for a siege and, most important, a fleet strong enough to stop any attempt to take off Cornwallis. On August 15 Washington learned that the last element was, incredibly, about to be supplied. The Comte de Grasse was bringing a large battle fleet up from the West Indies and would be off the Chesapeake Capes in early September. Moving more quickly than one would have thought possible, the first American units left for the South on August 19, followed presently by the French. As he moved across New Jersey, Washington constantly fretted about the possibility of de Grasse's not arriving in time; "I am distressed beyond expression. . . . I am almost all impatience and anxiety." On September 5 Rochambeau and his staff, sailing down the Delaware, were amazed to see Washington jumping and waving on the dock at Chester; they understood the loss of his usual composure when he told them what a special messenger had just told him: de Grasse was off the Capes of the Chesapeake! With some superb staff work, both armies moved men and materiel along until the men from the north joined the Pennsylvania Line, under Lafayette's command, at Williamsburg, twenty miles from Yorktown. By the time the northern armies arrived, de Grasse had fought and won the Battle of the Chesapeake Capes on September 9; this not only gave the allies a temporary but essential naval supremacy, it also covered the arrival of the Newport fleet with the vital siege guns. Incredibly, all the various pieces had been fitted together; the finished puzzle showed an English army of 8,000, with some supporting transport vessels bottled up at Yorktown.

What followed was almost anticlimactic. The siege, conducted mainly by the French who had the necessary equipment and expertise, was opened on September 28; Cornwallis resisted it sluggishly, almost fatalistically, and made no attempt to break through the allied lines. With the lines drawn close about his camp and the fire of more than 100 cannon concentrated on it, the English general proposed the opening of negotiations on the morning of October 17. Two days later, one-quarter of England's forces in North America were surrendered to Washington in a ceremony the like of which had not been seen since Saratoga, just four years earlier.[20]

Although Yorktown did not take away from the English the ability to mount another offensive, it proved to be the last major action of the war. Magnified by defeats in Florida, India, and elsewhere, plus the fact that this had been made possible by seapower, precisely where the English believed themselves invincible, Yorktown brought about a loss of nerve by the English and they began seriously to negotiate a peace treaty.[21] Washington reacted to the victory with his habitual caution, calling it "an interesting event that may be productive of much good . . ., but if it should be the means of relaxation . . . it had better not had happened."

Suiting action to words, the commander busied himself until early November cleaning up the odds and ends of the victory, seeing prisoners off to nearby camps, diverting captured materiel to convenient storehouses, and the like. After a short stay at Mount Vernon, he reached Philadelphia before the end of the month. He and Martha spent the winter there, the general conferring with the Congress and planning for the 1782 campaign, and both of them being lionized by the smart set of the Republic's capital. Recent administrative reforms in the Congress had lightened the work customarily thrust on Washington, especially the decision to appoint a full-time Superintendent of Finance, Robert Morris, a Philadelphia merchant. Morris let out contracts for army provisions to civilian contractors who, in the long run, fed the army better than it had ever been fed before (considering how it had been fed, that is not saying too much). A Secretary at War, Benjamin Lincoln, was made responsible for many of the decisions regarding the officer corps which the general previously had to make. Ironically, just as the war was winding down, the Congress was learning how to do its job properly.

In March Martha went home and Washington established headquarters in Newburgh, near the encampment at New Windsor, New York. There the spring and summer passed quietly. Yorktown had proved one thing, significant victories could be won only with the assistance of French sea power, and de Grasse's fleet was no more, having been defeated in an action off Guadeloupe in April. In August the new English commander in New York City, Sir Guy Carleton, offered to open negotiations on the Loyalists because a definitive peace treaty was then being negotiated in Paris. After the Congress denied this, Washington published the denial in a general order, adding what had become an almost—except for its obvious truth— monotonous caution: "The readiest way to procure a lasting and honorable peace is to be fully prepared vigorously to prosecute war." But war seemed to be the last thing on Carleton's mind as he notified Washington in September that fighting was suspended as far as he was concerned. Although he refused to accept the unilateral suspension, Washington lacked the means to undertake any large-scale action, especially after Rochambeau took his troops home in the fall. After his inactive summer, the general prophesied to Lafayette, "The winter will be tranquil."

Prophecy was never his strong suit. Since the early years of the war, the officers had complained about their conditions of service and Washington had spent many anxious hours soothing them and petitioning the Congress to redress their real grievances. The most important of these was their pay, which, even if it had been remitted promptly, was made ludicrously inadequate by the depreciation of the Continental currency. The Congress had promised half-pay pensions but lacked the means to redeem its word, especially after Rhode Island had rejected a proposal to give it taxing power. In March 1783 their resentment boiled over and some overt action, probably a call to the army not to disband until justice had been done it, seemed imminent. Plans for this were made with the connivance, possibly even at the instigation, of some nationalists in Philadelphia primarily interested in strengthening the Congress, not compensating the army. An anonymous call for an officers' meeting at New Windsor on March 12 precipitated Washington into action. He postponed the meeting until the fifteenth; then he addressed the officers personally, appealing to them to have faith in the Congress and themselves and act so that posterity could say, "Had this day been wanting, the world had never seen the last stage of perfection to which human nature is capable of attaining." Then he began to read a Congressman's letter, telling of recent action on their behalf; finding the writing too small to read, he took out his reading glasses, apologizing: "Gentlemen, you must pardon me. I have grown gray in your service and now find myself growing blind." He then left, and the officers adopted a resolution expressing their faith in the Congress. Washington had handled the affair magnificently; probably suspecting the nationalists' hand in the business, he nevertheless treated it as strictly an army affair and brought out of it vindication of civilian control of the military. The significance of the incident is hard to evaluate since it lies in the fact that certain things did not happen; Thomas Jefferson put it very well: "The moderation and virtue of a single character has probably prevented this revolution from being closed as most others have been by a subversion of the liberty it was intended to establish."[22]

Less than a month later, Washington was able to announce the signing of a preliminary treaty, urging the men to stay to their duty, "to preserve a perfect unvarying consistency of character through the very last act," as he feared they might begin deserting, believing the war over. But they stayed the course as they were gradually furloughed during the spring, taking with them certificates of service and their muskets, a gift from the Congress which could not give them their back pay. By June only the three-year men were left, waiting as impatiently as Washington for the English to evacuate New York City, their last garrison in the thirteen states. With the leisure to contemplate a United States at peace, Washington decided to issue the last of his circular letters to the governors of the states. In this address, known as "Washington's Legacy," he urged the strengthening of the Congress as the only hope for the future stability of the Republic. "For, according to the system of Policy the States shall adopt at this moment, they will stand or fall . . . for with our fate will the destiny of unborn Millions be involved." Thus, although the general rejected the nationalists' means, he agreed with their goal, a stronger Congress to hold the states together. Despite his prestige, the message was rejected as an intrusion into affairs which did not concern him. For now, the "Legacy" would be unredeemed.

The summer of 1783 passed by in unaccustomed leisure. A trip to Lake Champlain with New York's governor, George Clinton, and a stay with the Congress then sitting in Trenton occupied his time until he learned that Carleton intended to evacuate New York City on November 23. By early November only the troops assigned to march into the city were left in service. Much as it had been formed, so was it discharged, in bits and pieces with no grand ceremony or splendid climax, just small groups of men leaving until there was no Continental Army.

Just two days behind schedule Washington took his small force into New York City to be welcomed by the state authorities who had moved in only a few hours before. The ships of the English rearguard were held in the harbor for several days by contrary winds so that the general was not free to leave until Friday, December 4. At noon he met with his officers for a brief and eloquent farewell; entering the upper room at Fraunces Tavern, he passed by the buffet of food and poured himself a glass of wine. When the others had followed suit, he lifted the glass and spoke: "With a heart full of love and gratitude, I now take leave of you. I most devoutly wish that your later days may be as prosperous and happy as your former have been glorious and honorable." Then, turning to Knox, he impetuously embraced him; after that all had to be, and were, embraced. Nothing was said as the general went to the door and lifted his hand in silent farewell; nor was there any acclaim as he walked to the ferry slip. The silence spoke volumes.

After a ceremony-plagued trip across New Jersey, Washington reached Philadelphia on December 8 and settled his accounts with the Congress's finance office, thence on to Annapolis, where the legislators were sitting. The formal surrender of his commission was scheduled for the twenty-third at noon. For what he expected to be the last formal act of his public life, the general had written an address in which he gave Providence and his fellow citizens most of the credit for the victory, then, pausing as if he could not continue, he bade "an Affectionate farewell to this August body under whose orders I have so long acted, I here offer my commission, and take my leave of all the employments of public life." Thomas Mifflin as President of the Congress accepted the commission and thanked the general and it was all over. As at Fraunces's, he turned and left, too moved to say anything more. Late the next afternoon he reined in his horse at Mount Vernon to receive the excited greetings of family and servants. George Washington, Esq., was home to stay.

Washington once suggested to Nathanael Greene that if historians dared to present the story of what had been accomplished by the Continental Army, "it is more than probable that posterity will bestow on their labors the epithet and marks of fiction." The general's contribution to that "fiction" was only a part, but a vital and irreplaceable part, of the story; one should not forget the labors of the Congress, the states, and the people and the mistakes of the English. These also are part of the story.

George Washington was not one of history's great generals, but he was one of its great military leaders; his skills were not those of the battlefield tactician; rather they were those of the military administrator and diplomat. His generalship consisted mainly of getting the army together and keeping it together, neither of them easily accomplished tasks. He always lacked one or more of the tools needed for victory, most especially, as things turned out, the command of the sea, which gave his enemy such mobility. The English lost control of the sea off the Chesapeake Capes for a few weeks in 1781 and lost the war. Provided with all the tools he needed, the Virginia planter might have proved himself to be one of the military geniuses of all time, but for the kind of war he did have to fight, with the poor support the Congress and states were able to provide, he had exactly the qualities needed to secure victory: patience, self-discipline, organizing ability, willingness to work hard, and faith in the eventual success of the struggle for independence. These qualities sustained him during the long nights spent writing, often in vain, to the Congress and to the governors for the provisions needed for his men, for the men themselves, for all the materiel of war so sorely needed but so seldom provided.

Washington also contributed to American success, in a sense, by just being there. When he was appointed commander-in-chief in 1775 he instantly became a symbol of the united will of the colonies to resist English tyranny. As the war dragged on, the symbolic value of

Washington increased, and he was never seriously challenged in this popularity by the Congress or any other American general. This public acclaim was especially appropriate, for it was the only compensation Washington desired. It was the tangible sign that he had come as close as any man can to the Stoic ideal of unselfish service to the people, that he had kept faith, both with himself and with the republic.

CHAPTER 4

Interlude on the Potomac, 1784–1789

Our affairs seem to be drawing to an awful crisis.

WASHINGTON tried to move back into the pleasantly busy routines of Mount Vernon as quickly as possible but the habits of the past eight years were not easily shaken; for some time he continued, upon waking up, to turn over in his mind all the things he had to do that day; then, realizing "that I was no longer a public man, nor had anything to do with public transactions," he would permit himself a more leisurely arising. Frequently the first sight he had on his morning rounds was of visitors coming down the drive, some well-remembered faces from the army, some with letters of introduction, some with no letters but with a strong desire to be able to say to their children that they had sat at table with *him*. For more than a year the Washingtons did not once sit down alone to dinner, and the host accurately described himself as running "a well resorted tavern." If the general had led the Congress's army for only one fee, the esteem of his fellow citizens, he was now paying the cost of that affection.

Although he never adverted to it, the cost of his hospitality may well have weighed upon Washington as he surveyed the state of his private finances. Despite his best work, Lund Washington's stewardship had not been able to prevent some deterioration of the estate during the war; further, some of his creditors had taken advantage of Washington's willingness to accept depreciated wartime currency to pay off notes far below their true value. But as his personal scrupulosity did not permit him to do the same thing, the end of the war found him considerably the loser. The confused state of the books prevented an accurate accounting, but he knew he was painfully short of ready cash. A year after the war's end, he was unable to lend his brother £500 and had to ask George Mason if he would make the loan as a personal favor.

The most immediate source of income would be the produce of Mount Vernon, and Washington continued the diligent cultivation and intelligent experimentation which had been such an unusual feature of his farming before the war. In good years he might have got as much as $10,000 to $15,000 without considering the use of the house and livestock, increase in slaves, etc. But not all years were good, and in 1798, even with the profits from a distillery and other enterprises on the farms, Mount Vernon yielded less than $4,500, or about 2.25 percent on an estimated value of $200,000. The Custis estates and the rents on his western properties, uncollected since before the war, constituted the rest of his income. Washington's farming knowledge was expanded by a correspondence with Arthur Young, the English agricultural reformer, begun in 1785. Young might have been the source of plans for a seed drill, built by slave artisans, which apparently worked only under ideal conditions. Elaborate tables of crop rotation were worked out, considering not only the market value of the crops, but also the labor involved and the benefit to the soil. Although Washington described Mount Vernon's soil as a "good loam," it was actually of rather poor quality and needed constant attention to be productive. One of Washington's more unusual enthusiasms was an attempt to popularize mules in America. The animal, a hybrid of the horse and the ass, worked harder than a horse while requiring less fodder and suffering from fewer diseases than his equine relative. Washington managed to breed into one jackass, "Compound," the size and strength of "Royal Gift" from the King of Spain and the liveliness and good humour of "Knight of Malta," a gift from Lafayette. Although mules never became as popular as Washington had hoped, their subsequent history justified his enthusiasm, and at his death Mount Vernon had two mules for every draft horse. Despite his steady interest and constant experimentation, Washington never considered himself an especially skillful farmer and in his last message to Congress as president he urged the establishment of a group to spread the kind of knowledge he had found so difficult to acquire.[1]

The principal labor force at Mount Vernon was, of course, slaves. During the war, Washington had come to appreciate the competence of free blacks serving in northern regiments and perhaps to doubt not only the efficiency but also the morality of slavery as a labor system. He does not seem to have been an especially kindly master, permitting his slaves to live in ramshackle quarters and speaking brusquely to them. But he did know them as individuals and tried to use them as their special competence and temperament indicated. One, Davy, served as manager of one of the Mount Vernon farms for years. Despite his respect for their competence, no special pains were taken to improve either the minds or the morals of the slaves. On several occasions during the 1780s he confided his misgivings about the system to friends and visitors, once commenting that he did not even want to think about the problem. However, he could not help but think about it, and with interesting results, to be noted later.[2]

In February 1784 Washington formally resigned from the vestry of his Anglican parish; since he seems to have regarded this as a civic, not a religious duty, it was not a sign of unwillingness to participate in a church as much as a sign of his retirement from public life. He was not hostile to religion but he was devoid of any deep personal religious faith. Much in the fashion of other eighteenth-century gentlemen, he considered religion as one of the important elements in the stability of American society; it was religion's "laudable endeavors to render men sober, honest, and good citizens, and the obedient subjects of a lawful government" which impressed him the most. Thus he approved of a Virginia law requiring all to pay a tax for the support of Christian churches; their work benefited all, even non-Christians, so all should pay. This opinion not only shows what moderns would consider an illiberal attitude toward religious liberty but also a utilitarian attitude toward religion itself. It was, however, thoroughly in keeping with the enlightened Deism of Washington's generation.[3]

Once he had Mount Vernon on the road to profitability, Washington began to look to the other parts of his estate; "having found it indispensably necessary to visit my Landed property West of the Apalachean [sic] Mountains," he traveled west in the fall of 1784. Almost immediately the trip took on another aspect as Washington began to survey the possibilities of opening up an easy water route between the Ohio and the Potomac. It was just as well he had a second task at hand as he managed to collect very little in back rents and even had to begin court suits to evict some squatters on land he owned in southwestern Pennsylvania, near Pittsburgh. That was as far west as he got, for reports of hostile activity by Indians near the bounty lands made a visit to them unwise. Home was reached on October 4, just a little more than a month after he had left.

Back at Mount Vernon, Washington put the material he had gathered on his trip west into a report to Richard Henry Lee, the

President of the Congress; in the report he returned to one of his favorite topics of the war years, the necessity of a stronger union. As he saw it, commerce and politics marched along nicely together; the West hangs "as it were on a pivot—the touch of a feather" could incline it either toward the East and allegiance with the United States or toward the West and independence with a connection with the Spanish in Louisiana or the English in Canada. Trade connections via an improved Potomac River would be one of the surest bonds of union with the pleasant dividend of increased trade throughout the Chesapeake area. But the "great object," as he confided it to Edmund Randolph, "is to connect the Western Territory with the Atlantic States; all others with me are secondary." The "great object" took definite form in May 1785 when Washington became president of the Potomac Company, jointly chartered by Virginia and Maryland to construct the much-desired water route; he resigned the office in 1789. [4]

As he viewed the country in the mid-1780s, it needed all the bonds of union which could be forged; the Congress, the states, and the people were all responsible for sinking "our national character much below par" and bringing the country to the point where "a step or two further must plunge us into a Sea of Troubles, perhaps anarchy and confusion." No prospect was all black; immediate action might forestall the impending disaster. And he did not doubt what the remedy was: "I do not conceive we can exist long as a nation without having lodged somewhere a power which will pervade the whole Union." Perhaps his greatest hope was in the people, for there was "virtue at the bottom." But something had to be done, for "affairs seem to be drawing to an awful crisis."

That this "awful crisis" might occur, Washington was firmly convinced, and a good many other Americans agreed with him. Many pressing problems—the Indians, and the English occupation of posts in New York and the Northwest, to name only two—were hanging fire because the Congress lacked the power to deal with them. But it also ought to be noted that the Congress was not the nation, that there was much prosperity to be found in the states and, in the areas where there was distress, the future was still bright. Further, in the agrarian economy of the late-eighteenth-century United States, farmers who complained about low prices for their produce still had food, shelter, and a rough but adequate existence. Many of the problems which Washington and others bemoaned were only potentially trouble-some, things which a great nation ought not to tolerate but which, more realistically, the United States of 1786 might well have to live with for a while. Further, the success of the government set up by the Constitution has masked the possibility that a reformed Articles of Confederation, especially one which gave Congress a source of revenue and effective control over commerce, could have been an adequate government for years to come.

Maryland and Virginia, in an attempt to iron out trade problems in the Chesapeake Bay area, held a meeting in March 1785. At Washington's invitation, the commissioners met at Mount Vernon (he was not a delegate) and achieved sufficient success to lead Virginia to issue a call to all the states to meet at Annapolis, Maryland, in September 1786 to discuss trade problems. This meeting drew delegations from only the middle states in addition to Virginia; the delegates decided not to attempt a settlement of the trade problems they had been convened to discuss but instead issued a report stating that they believed the Union's problems were sufficiently grave to justify a general meeting of the states in Philadelphia the following May. Copies were sent to the Congress and all the states. This bare recital of facts hides a good bit of activity by those who wanted to strengthen the Union,—Federalists, as they were soon to call themselves. They, as well as those who wanted to preserve the weak union of the Articles, or at least resist change, knew that Washington's opinion would count for much with the people should a strong movement to strengthen the Congress develop. Anyone who had written or spoken with Washington knew his opinion on it; his convictions on what had to be done to keep the country strong would hardly keep him from attending the proposed meeting.[5]

Rather, the obstacles came from Washington's sense of his own honor and from circumstances. He construed his promise to retire from public life, made at the war's end, to be a bar to any kind of public office. But as an index of his strong convictions on the necessity of some kind of drastic reform, he left the door open should the country voice "its affection and confidence"; in other words, he would accept a draft. Then an additional complication was introduced; the Society of the Cincinnati, an hereditary fraternity of ex–Continental Army officers, was also meeting in Philadelphia in May 1787. Because some had objected to the society, especially its hereditary character, Washington had proposed reforms which the state chapters had rejected. Using poor health and his own business as excuses, he had already sent his regrets; now, how could he attend without being disrespectful to the Cincinnati? Although he did not want to be associated with what was seen as aristocracy and privilege, neither did he want to insult gratuitously some well-meaning ex-comrades.

His nomination by Virginia to head its delegation in late 1786 gave a point to his dilemma, but Governor Randolph wisely decided not to press him for an answer immediately; the matter could be left to ripen a bit. Events elsewhere conspired to speed up the ripening process. In western Massachusetts, farmers under the leadership of Daniel Shays resisted the collection of heavy taxes and, for a time, seemed about to stop the processes of government. As reported to him, this very much alarmed Washington and he seemed briefly to despair that Americans were capable of self-government. Now the point of his reservations came to be: should he use his influence to support a meeting that may be poorly attended and ineffectual? In February 1787 the Congress officially sanctioned the call, and the meeting's chances of success became much greater—indeed, in Washington's judgment, perhaps "the last peaceable mode of essaying the practicability" of the present government. There was a selfish element in Washington's anxiety here; he seemed unwilling to expend what he prized most highly, his public reputation, even in helping to preserve the independence and integrity of the Union. But the time had come to make a decision, and in April he accepted his state's call to go to Philadelphia. Now that the battle line had been drawn, he wanted the meeting to "adopt no temporizing expedient, but probe the defects of the constitution to the bottom and provide *radical cures* [emph. added];" whether its suggestions were adopted or not, it would "be looked to as a luminary, which sooner or later will shed its influence." Everything should be risked, for everything was at stake.

Monday, May 14, found only two states' delegations in attendance at the state house in Philadelphia, where the meeting was to be held. Washington filled the time with, as it seemed to him, idle socializing until the twenty-fifth, when a quorum was present and the meeting could organize itself. It is unnecessary to repeat the day-to-day proceedings of the Convention here, not only because that story has been well told elsewhere but also because Washington, aside from his formal presidency of the meeting, spoke from the floor only once during the long, hot summer. At the very end, he asked the delegates to reduce the minimum size of electoral districts of the House of Representatives to 30,000 people, stating that government should be as close to the people as possible. The Convention unanimously agreed. Since Washington kept the secrecy of the meeting so closely that he did not enter any comments about its proceedings in his journal, his desires on the form of the new government can only be inferred from some of his votes within his state's delegation (each state had one vote, cast as a majority of its delegates decided).

Although Washington has never been known as a political theorist, he did have several well-considered principles which he applied to political affairs. Government had to be strong, so he voted to suppress the states' interests; the executive had to be strong also so Washington voted in favor of a single executive and one not elected by, and thus dependent on, the legislature; he also approved making a three-fourths rather than two-thirds vote of the Congress necessary to override an executive veto, but he lost on the last point. And, as his request on the size of House districts indicated, he wanted government to be close to the people. Other than these few rules, however, he seemed to be ready to accept any "tolerable compromise" that would strengthen the Union and restrain the states from excesses.[6]

Washington's contribution to the success of the Convention, therefore, was not in the work of drafting a new Constitution. It lay in his simply being there; that he attended, presided, and signed the result of the Convention convinced countless Americans of the value of the new Constitution. Further, he may have helped to shape the presidency in the new government, for as it became obvious that the executive was to be entrusted to one person some of the delegates, expecting Washington to be the first president, were content to leave some features of the office vague or to give it more strength than it might otherwise have received. Further definition could safely be left to him.

The Convention finished its work on September 17 and the members left for their homes, most to help secure their state's ratification of the Constitution, some few to oppose it. In this contest Washington played a discreet role typified by the covering letter he enclosed with copies to other Virginians:

I wish the Constitution which is offered had been made more perfect, but I sincerely believe it is the best that could be obtained at this time; and, as a constitutional door is opened for amendment hereafter, the adoption of it under the present circumstances of the Union is, in my opinion desirable.

This basic argument, expanded and sometimes modified to suit the recipient, was used over and over again as he kept up his large correspondence. No objection was made when some of his letters were printed in the newspapers except when he did not expect this and fretted about the clumsy style of what he thought of as a strictly private letter. All in all, he successfully walked the line between backing the document he had helped write and not appearing to be running for the presidency.

For, during the contest, many referred to their confident expectation that Washington would accept the position. But over and above this was his obvious approval of the new frame of government. The only way to counter it was to discredit either his judgment or his integrity, and few attempted to do that. James Monroe certainly claimed too much when he said that Washington's "influence carried this government," but, equally certain, his approval, his probable presidency, and his cautious campaigning were substantial advantages for the Federalists as they carried the Constitution successfully through the ratification contest. That contest ended late in July 1788 when New York, as the eleventh state, ratified; Rhode Island almost ignored the process from beginning to end and North Carolina had adjourned its convention without coming to a final decision. Be that as it may, more than the requisite nine states had ratified, and whether the two hold-outs joined sooner or later, the Constitution was going into effect, and with a good chance of success, for, as Washington predicted:

When the people shall find themselves secure under an energetic government, when foreign nations shall be disposed to give us equal advantages in commerce from dread of retaliation, when the burdens of war shall be in a manner done away by the sale of western lands; when the seeds of happiness which are sewn here shall begin to expand themselves, and when every one (under his own vine and fig tree) shall begin to taste the fruits of freedom; then all these blessings (for all these blessings will come) will be referred to the fostering influence of the new government.

But then, more realistically, he added: "Whereas many causes will have conspired to produce them." For many reasons the grand experiment in self-government which, for Washington, had started on the heights overlooking Boston in 1775 was going to receive a fair trial.

Now that the trial was about to begin, Washington would have to make up his mind on a question that had been hovering in the background, sometimes popping to the surface, since the Convention: the presidency. He had good personal reasons for wanting to stay at Mount Vernon, not the least of which was the place itself; in addition, he wondered if the Antifederalists who had opposed the

Constitution would accept him and how people generally would view his breaking of his 1783 promise to retire from public life. In his consideration of the problem, he nicely balanced duty and reputation: nothing would take him away from Mount Vernon "unless it be a *conviction* that the partiality of my countrymen had made my services absolutely necessary, joined to a *fear* that my refusal might induce a belief that I preferred the conservation of my own reputation and private ease to the good of my country [orig. emph.]." But in the end the choice was more or less made for him; when he heard that the strongly Antifederalist Governor of New York, George Clinton, was being considered for vice-president, he let it be known that he considered John Adams much the better man for the job. If he was concerned about the vice-presidency sufficiently to influence the choice of its occupant, how could he refuse the presidency? Thus there was no grand announcement of his willingness to accept the call of his fellow citizens, just a slow, steady march of events until he silently or at least implicitly accepted what had become inevitable. Since there would be no formal notice until March at the earliest, he did not have to make any statement when he learned in mid-February that enough states had voted for him to make certain his election. His acceptance could be seen in the preparations he started to make for the move to New York, where the new government would be seated: a last visit to his mother; instructions to George Augustine Washington, his nephew and manager; the sending of Tobias Lear, his personal secretary, to the capital in early April. After these steps had been taken, no one near him could have been surprised at his answer when Charles Thomson, the Secretary of the Congress, handed him a formal notice of his election on April 14. In the gracefully phrased reply, he bowed to "this fresh proof of my country's esteem and confidence" and informed Thomson he would be ready to leave for New York in two days. The furlough was over; the next campaign had begun.

CHAPTER 5

A Commission from the People, 1789–1793

So much is expected, so many untoward circumstances may intervene, in such a new and critical situation, that I feel an insuperable diffidence in my own abilities.

AS the president-elect began his journey to the new government's capital on April 16, he confided to his diary that his mind was "oppressed with more anxious and painful sensations than I have words to express." This was certainly true, but it was also probably true that he half-welcomed his new position. What better proof of the public's esteem, of the security of his reputation than his election to the presidency without a dissenting vote? The journey to New York City was punctuated with dozens of demonstrations of the public's affection, reaffirming the official decision of the Electoral College. No crossroads village could let Washington through without at least a parade of militia and, if possible, an artillery salute. One of the most elaborate welcomes was staged, fittingly enough, by the nation's largest city, Philadelphia, but the ceremony which seemed to affect Washington the most occurred in one of the smaller cities, Trenton, New Jersey. There the bridge over the Assunpink Creek had been decorated with thirteen bunting-bedecked arches (despite the fact that Rhode Island and North Carolina still had not ratified), the same bridge where the general had sat his horse in January 1777 while he watched Colonel Edward Hand's men delay Cornwallis's vanguard. Now, in the warm spring sunshine, thirteen girls dressed in white sang:

> Virgins fair and matrons grave,
> Those thy conquering arm did save.
> Build for thee celestial bowers,
> Strew your hero's way with flowers.

And they strew. As sentimental as the words might seem, they had a powerful effect on Washington, for he wrote a thank-you note to the choir that evening in which he explicitly referred to the contrast between the scene that day and 1777. This is unusual, perhaps unique, for he had a habit of visiting sites connected with the war—Valley Forge during the Philadelphia Convention, for instance—but not recording the memories, if any, which the visit stirred up. Unbeknownst to them, the Trenton choir had stirred him deeply and strongly.[1]

The climax of the journey came on April 23 when Washington and his party reached Elizabeth, where they were met by a delegation representing both the Congress and the State of New York. The President-elect boarded a specially built barge manned by thirteen master pilots of the port and was rowed through Newark Bay and across the Hudson to the city. Other vessels fell in behind as the barge moved along; one sloop was filled with singers who serenaded the presidential party with songs of the type—and quality—heard in Trenton. As Washington stepped out of the barge at the Battery in New York City, he was greeted cordially by Governor George Clinton. The welcome of the strongly Antifederal Clinton seemed to be a good omen for the future of the new government. Washington was escorted through a tightly pressing crowd to a house set aside for his use, to rest and prepare for a banquet that evening. The prevailing sentiment seemed to be typified by a line heard frequently throughout the day: "Well, he deserves it all."[2]

But that referred to the past; the future was what interested Washington. He readily agreed to the Congress's arrangements for the inauguration: April 30 would be the date, and the refurbished City Hall, now christened Federal Hall, where the Congress sat, would be the site. The day proved to be bright, clear, and mild—another good omen for the future? At 12:30 a coach and four pulled away from the presidential mansion; its occupant wore a suit cut from cloth manufactured in the United States, the buttons decorated with an eagle to complete the patriotic motif. At Federal Hall, he was formally introduced to the Congress, gathered in the second-floor Senate chamber, by Vice-President Adams, who had already been sworn in. He then stepped out onto a balcony where, in the absence of any federal judicial officials, Robert R. Livingston, Chancellor of the State of New York, administered the oath of office. At its conclusion, Livingston gestured as if he were presenting the new president to the people and exclaimed: "Long live George Washington, President of the United States!" The crowd, quiet only for the oath-taking, broke into loud cheers, punctuated by church bells and a thirteen-gun salute.

The presidential party then moved inside for the Inaugural Address, a brief and general speech of about 1,200 words. Washington referred to the seriousness of his task and requested pardon in advance for any unintentional errors. Evidence was given that the United States was being guided by the "Almighty Being" who directs human affairs—for example, "the important revolution" just accomplished "through the tranquil deliberations and voluntary consent" of the people. The Congress needed no guidance from him as to necessary legislation and he was certain "no local prejudices or attachments, no separate views nor party animosities" would divert them from their work (he would not always be certain of this). He made only two specific suggestions: the Congress should consider recommending amendments to the Constitution to correct deficiencies pointed to by some during the ratification controversy. This would result in the passage of the Bill of Rights, the first ten amendments. He also requested that his compensation, following his wartime practice, would be confined to his expenses only. Then came a brief statement imploring the blessings of the "benign Parent of the Human Race" on the Republic and the speech was over. One observer, Senator William Maclay of Pennsylvania, noted the awkwardness of the president in delivering the speech and mourned that he was not first in speechmaking as in everything else.[3] But the public aspect of the presidency was probably the most painful to Washington, especially the speechmaking, and he never improved substantially in it. A thanksgiving service at St. Paul's Church followed. After a private dinner, Washington toured the city with his secretaries, Lear and David Humphreys, his old wartime aide, to view the fireworks and illuminations at the end of the day's celebrations.

Festivities over, Washington settled down to his share of the work of forming the new government. What Washington and the Congress were attempting was a novel enterprise: the self-conscious formation of a new government based on popular consent, what no one before them had tried to do and what few after them would do so successfully. Washington realized the importance of everything he did. "Few who are not philosophical spectators can realize the difficult and delicate part which a man in my situation had to act. . . . I walk on untrodden ground. There is scarcely any part of my conduct which may not hereafter be drawn into precedent." For governments are not formed simply of taxes and armies and bureaus; even the most trivial aspects of Washington's behavior were anxiously observed by people concerned not only with the substance, but also the accidents of the new government.

The President of the United States then occupied a unique position; there was no other elected head of state in the European world. The House and Senate had already disagreed over how to address the president, with the upper house wanting to send its reply to the Inaugural Address to "His Highness, the President of the United States of America, and Protector of their Liberties," but the House stood firm on "To the President of the United States." In spoken discourse, Washington was addressed as "Your Excellency," as he had been during the war. Blending advice solicited from various quarters as to how he should entertain, Washington decided to hold a weekly reception at which all informal, social visits would be made; this would give him the time he needed for his official business and appointments while at the same time permitting any decently dressed individual a chance to speak with the president. Mrs. Washington held a similar reception on Friday evenings for the ladies; Washington usually attended this also. Observing the president at these gatherings, Abigail Adams, the vice-president's wife, was impressed with his happy "Faculty of appearing to accommodate and yet carrying his point. . . . He is polite with dignity, affable without familiarity, distant without Haughtiness, Grave without Austerity." Hers seems to have been a minority viewpoint, or else he was more relaxed with the ladies than at his own receptions, which were usually more crowded with strangers. Every Thursday government officials—congressmen, generally—attended a formal dinner; these were culinary triumphs but could be social disasters, at least if Senator Maclay is to be believed, but the Senator had come to New York sniffing suspiciously for stray scents of aristocracy and monarchy and was not to be disappointed.[4]

The grave, formal tone of the administration, thought necessary by Washington so that the new government not seem cheap or familiar, was also a reflection of the public mask which he customarily wore as a disguise for his own shyness and feelings during occasions which were uncomfortable for him. He relaxed only with a few old friends at Mount Vernon. But Maclay was not the only one to feel that the tone was excessively formal, and by 1790 even Virginians were making barbed comments about the aristocratic airs of the Republican Court. Although the President did not worry about the formality of his administration, he was concerned about his limited social circle and, before his first term ended, he asked Tobias Lear to give him impressions of public opinion as his secretary mixed with all kinds of different people, many more "than could fall to the lot of a stationary character who is always revolving in a particular circle." Unfortunately, Washington would not always see this as a problem.

Congress decided to ignore Washington's request about his compensation, reasoning that the office should not be tailored to wishes of one person, and gave the president a salary of $25,000 a year. Washington, however, treated this as if it were compensation for expenses and had Lear enter the salary paid against expenses accruing. Since he always spent more than his salary, some years as much as $5,000 more, he always drew the total amount. As Mount Vernon's expenses were lower in his absence, this was no great burden, and the flow of cash from his salary may actually have helped his personal finances. The heavy expenses of his household were increased by Washington's decision to live as "respectably" as circumstances permitted. Fifteen to twenty servants, supplemented when the Congress was in session, were employed in the house and stables; as many as seven slaves from Mount Vernon might also be used, but they did not work where the public would see them. During 1790 the expenses of the table alone ran to about $165 a week, with an additional $1,700 a year being spent for wine, cider, etc.; these expenses remained about the same during Washington's presidency. All in all, the president adhered closely to his intention of giving the office, in its social aspects as dignified an air as was possible despite the protests of some anxious democrats that this "squinted" toward aristocracy and monarchy.[5]

Still, there was something to the tone of the administration, at least as it was reported in the press, to give a thoughtful citizen pause as he viewed the new government. The Federalist press used only superlatives in reporting the president's actions and did not stint in awarding honorific titles. Martha was usually styled "Lady Washington," as well as the wives of others prominent in the administration, no matter how humble their origins. The silliness, as well as the falseness, of much of this reporting is illustrated in the *Federal Gazette's* description of Washington's reaction to a popular melodrama, *The Maid of the Mill* "the great and good Washington manifested his approbation of this interesting part of the opera by the tribute of a tear." Although retrospect shows that there was little to fear from this, contemporaries might be pardoned their anxiety; as Jefferson later noted:

hangers-on "had wound up the ceremonials of the government to a pitch of stateliness which nothing but [Washington's] personal character could have supported, and which no character after him could maintain." And it says much for Washington's conduct of the presidency that most of the criticism directed at him concerned just such relatively trivial aspects of the office as its social tone.[6]

For, if government was more than taxes and armies and bureaus, it was those things also. Although the secretaries of the old Congress continued in office, its rudimentary executive organization could not long serve the expanded tasks of the new government. In congressmen's eyes, revenue came first, and a bill levying tariffs on imports and a tonnage tax on all ships entering American ports was presented to the president early in July. As originally drafted the rates would have discriminated against English goods and ships in retaliation for their discrimination against America's, but this provision was taken out. While the President would have liked to see England receive a taste of the power of the new government, he had decided that his veto could be used only on constitutional questions, so although he disagreed with the policy of the bill, he signed it on July 4, 1789. What more appropriate way to celebrate the thirteenth anniversary of American independence than with a demonstration of the new power of republican government?

The Congress gave the president three executive departments to assist him. A Department of State was to handle both domestic and foreign affairs; the War Department would take up the work of its predecessor and a Treasury Department was to take in hand the complex task of bringing order to the nation's finances. An attorney-general, to act as the government's chief legal officer, was also provided as was a rudimentary system of federal courts, capped by a six-man Supreme Court. The Congress's work done, Washington's began as he tried to find suitable men to fill these posts. War was the easiest, as Henry Knox was willing to continue in this post which he had filled for the old Congress. Washington readily appointed him. John Jay, who had been secretary for foreign affairs in the old government, was appointed to head the Supreme Court; he had recently proposed closing the Mississippi to American commerce in a treaty with the Spanish, and Washington might have feared that western animosity toward him would keep him from being an effective secretary. In filling the other posts on the courts and elsewhere, Washington paid attention not only to legal qualifications but also to sectional distribution. Although Washington did not intend to be partisan, he was not going to ignore the obvious sectional feeling in the country. After Jay, the two obvious choices for the State Department were John Adams and Thomas Jefferson, but the former's occupancy of the vice-presidency ruled him out. Although Jefferson was then serving as American minister in Paris, he was coming home for a leave late in the year and Washington waited until then to ask him to take the post. Even then, it took a combination of several letters and a personal visit before Jefferson said yes. Jay filled in until he took up the post in March 1790. Although they had not associated much, both Washington and Jefferson had served in the prewar Burgesses and came from the Virginia gentry, so, in a way, they knew each other very well. Calling as it did for a combination of fiscal competence and statesmanship, the head of the Treasury Department should have been one of the more difficult posts to fill, but Washington had frequently spoken of appointing his wartime aide Hamilton, and, as soon as the department was formed, appointed him. Edmund Randolph as attorney-general completed Washington's official family. The president knew all of the men reasonably well and expected a harmonious relationship to develop among them.

Not only merit and sectionalism were considered when appointments were being made. Wherever possible, Washington practiced a kind of crude "veterans' preference" and gave positions to those who had fought for independence, but this alone would not qualify anyone for a position. In only one case were political factors considered. Rhode Island finally entered the Union in May 1790 (North Carolina had come in the previous November) and in that state Washington consciously appointed those who had worked for the ratification of the Constitution. Elsewhere, the individual decisions were based on a combination of "suitable qualifications, personal merit, and former services." All in all, an acceptable set of criteria.[7]

Washington had a clear view of the role his secretaries were to play in administration. He wrote: "The impossibility that one man should be able to perform all the great business of the State, I take to have been the reason for instituting the great Departments, and appointing officers therein, to assist the supreme Magistrate in discharging the duties of his trust." Thus the secretaries were his agents, to perform whatever tasks he saw fit to assign to them. So in addition to presiding over his department, a secretary might find himself doing anything from giving advice on all sorts of matters to writing a state paper. If the variety of their work blurred the lines of responsibility,

Washington did not become concerned, as he viewed administration as a kind of communal enterprise; a gain for one was a gain for all. He kept track of what they were doing within their respective departments by reading all letters going out over a Secretary's signature along with the letters they were answering; thus

he was always in accurate possession of all facts and proceedings in every part of the Union, and to whatsoever department they related; he formed a central point for the different branches; preserved a unity of object and action among them; exercised that participation in the suggestion of affairs which his office made incumbent on him; and met himself the due responsibility for whatever was done.

While Washington readily assumed responsibility for what his assistants did, he did not interfere in their work. When the French minister, the Comte de Moustier, tried to approach him directly, the diplomat was coolly informed that the president believed it to be the practice "in most polished nations . . . that business should be digested and prepared by the Heads" of departments. He early conceived of the Cabinet as a unit and, on several occasions, authorized it to take action should an emergency arise in his absence. But meetings of all the secretaries with the president were usually restricted to serious matters, and only five meetings were held during the first term. When the wars of the French Revolution began to complicate American foreign policy, meetings were called more frequently. By this time, April 1793, Randolph also attended and Adams had stopped coming. These meetings were confined to policy questions; administrative matters were handled between the president and the relevant secretary.[8]

In keeping with his wartime practice, Washington did not confine himself to his official advisors; rather he canvassed widely and then considered the various answers, sometimes at length, before coming to a decision. Thus not only the Cabinet, but also Adams and Jay were consulted on how to treat an informal emissary from the English who presented himself in July 1790. Madison was asked for guidance on a minor point of constitutional interpretation and in 1792, when Washington was considering retiring, the Virginia congressman drafted a farewell message.[9] In addition to general news from correspondents, especially how the government was seen by the people, the president often asked individuals about someone in their locale who was being considered for an appointment.

Although at first glance Washington's decision-making procedures seem to be unsystematic, he followed a general rule of involving only as many people as were needed to arrive at a sound, well-buttressed conclusion. And when he made up his mind, that was the end of the debate, if there had even been one. If a Cabinet vote was called for, which was not often, he almost always followed the result; with a Cabinet containing two men of such surpassing ability as Jefferson and Hamilton, along with their competent associates, a majority decision was likely to be a sound one.

As it happened, Hamilton's responsibilities were in an area Washington was unfamiliar with and also involved primarily congressional action; the Secretary of the Treasury worked alone or with congressmen directly. Further, in forming the department, Congress had given itself the right to call on the secretary to "digest and prepare" reports on fiscal matters, thus they had a kind of private line with each other which bypassed the president. Jefferson's responsibilities, on the other hand, involved issues which had to be settled primarily within the executive branch and which had to represent policies generally agreed upon; also Washington had pronounced opinions in foreign affairs. Thus Jefferson's work was more likely to involve close work with the president and could be undone by a Cabinet vote. As disagreements developed between the two principal secretaries, they were exacerbated by these circumstances. Washington's hope of a happy official family was not to be fulfilled.

The president's relations with the Congress were relatively harmonious, in part at least because he did not see himself as involved in the legislative process. As noted, he believed he could veto a bill only on grounds of unconstitutionality. Thus Congress did not have to consider the president's wishes as they debated; as long as the bill was not clearly unconstitutional, they were certain it would be signed. This was not only Washington's opinion. When Jefferson argued that the bill chartering the First Bank of the United States was unconstitutional, he concluded by stating that if the president were not perfectly convinced of this, he should sign the bill out of respect for the judgment of Congress.[10] This narrow conception of the veto did not mean that Washington was completely passive toward Congress; rather, he saw the Constitution as a relatively detailed guide for him: he could recommend, via his annual messages, areas which needed legislative attention, which could be supplemented by special messages if necessary; but he did not have the right to interfere in Congress's deliberations. While important measures were being considered, he did not speak or write of them lest his views influence the legislators. But he could give the Congress a message; when Hamilton, in a report to Congress, recommended a system of bounties to help build up manufacturing, Washington did not mention the report in his messages and only later commented that he thought the bounties would be both ineffective and unconstitutional. The report was never acted upon.

He took full advantage of his right to advise the Congress and gave them a long shopping list in his First Annual Message, January 1790, when he recommended improvement of the army and militia, support of manufactures, improved roads, and, especially, the necessity of promoting education, among other topics. The message was delivered personally to Congress with ceremony Washington must have approved, for he noted the details carefully in his diary. His general conception of the president had him as the first magistrate, not the first lawgiver, of the nation.

Experience disclosed that the Constitution was not so clear in other areas. In August 1789 Washington and Secretary Knox went to the Senate to seek their "advice and consent" on instructions for commissioners being sent to negotiate a treaty with the Southern Indians (Indian affairs were the province of the War Department). The Senate proved unable to deliberate in the presence of the president and Senator Maclay recommended that the matter be referred to a select committee. At this Washington exclaimed: "*This defeats every purpose of my coming here* [orig. emph.]" and explained that he had brought Knox along so that the instructions could be considered expeditiously. By mutual consent, the business was put over to the following Monday. But the overly suspicious Maclay "knew" that the president had come down only to overawe the Senate with his presence: "Form only will be left to us. This will not do with Americans." And he reported the president as leaving "with a discontented air. Had it been any other man than the man whom I wish to regard as the first character in the world, I would have said, with sullen dignity." Monday's session went no better than the first and, as Washington left, he was reported as saying that he would be "damned" if he ever went "there" again. And, of course, no president ever has gone "there" and the Senate can only consent to a treaty already negotiated by the executive; the advice clause has become a dead letter and treaties are negotiated with a free hand by the president.[11]

Washington was responsible for another diminution of the Senate's power in foreign relations when, in October 1789, he asked Gouver-

neur Morris, then in Europe on business, to go to London and
informally ascertain the English government's views on a number of
points left over or inadequately dealt with by the peace treaty.
(Neither the United States nor England had a minister in the other's
capital.) Although this weakened the constitutional prerogative of the
Senate to approve all persons nominated to represent the country
abroad, Morris's negative report, received in July 1790, permitted
the administration to take a strong line with an informal emissary
from England who came to New York later that summer.

Thus by a combination of careful attention to the Constitution,
discreet departures from it, continuation of old practices, and trial
and error, the Constitution was being fleshed out and put into
execution. By the time of his First Message to Congress, the
government had a revenue, the executive departments had been
established, and, with the exception of State, manned; attention was
being paid to foreign relations and Congress was presently to take up
the area where the most improvement was needed, the unpaid debt
left over from the War for Independence. Washington may justifiably
have taken personal satisfaction when he congratulated Congress in
his message "on the present favorable prospects of our public affairs."

With this optimistic judgment down, Washington looked forward
to a kind of vacation during the congressional recess. He had decided
to tour the New England states "to acquire knowledge of the face of
the Country, the growth and agriculture thereof—and the temper
and disposition of the inhabitants toward the new government."
Accompanied by his secretaries and some servants, he left New York
on October 15 and traveled through Connecticut, Massachusetts,
and New Hampshire, avoiding the still-obstinate Rhode Island, for
almost a month. He carefully noted in his journal not only the
condition of the roads, style of cultivation and the like but also
extensive information on commerce and manufacturing, showing his
realization that even these strange ways of making a living figured in
the nation's prosperity. Also into the journal went an unconsciously
amusing recounting of Massachusetts Governor John Hancock's
abortive attempt to upstage the president by receiving the first visit,
"which he knew was improper." The affair ended with Hancock being
melodramatically carried into Washington's presence to maintain the
governor's claim of being too ill to call. This minor annoyance aside,
the rest of the trip went well and Washington did not even object too
strongly to being marooned in a Connecticut town by the state's blue
laws although he had to spend the Sunday listening to two "very

lame" sermons by the local parson. He made a similar tour of the South in the spring of 1791, when he also attempted to learn the people's reaction to Hamilton's funding plan which had just been enacted. If the new government was to gain the loyalty of its citizens, if a sense of American nationalism was to evolve, just such expedients as this were necessary. As Jefferson noted, one of Washington's chief functions for the new nation was to serve as the focus for loyalty until a less personal, more general feeling could develop. The tours helped to fulfill that function in the most effective way possible, by the hero's presence.

While the government seemed to be going well, all was not good in Washington's personal life. His mother died during the summer of 1789 of breast cancer; in consoling his sister, he intimated that their mother was now more comfortable than she had been for some time past, one of the few indications he ever gave that he believed in a life after death. Nor was Washington as healthy as he wished; he suffered a painful abcess on his thigh during the summer of 1789 and during the following winter was stricken with a cold which developed into pneumonia. After he apparently lingered between life and death for a week, the fever broke and he quickly recovered. Fatalistically he commented that such things came in threes; his next illness would probably carry him off. While he was not plagued by ill health during his presidency, he was in markedly poorer health than during the war, when the physical and mental demands had probably been greater. The difference might be explained as much by his inability to exercise as by his advancing age; he had constantly to work off the tensions of his office by horseback-riding and other forms of exercise which had been an integral part of his wartime duties. Physically, the only feature which visitors commented on was his teeth, which had been poor for years and were now almost completely gone, being replaced by a variety of dentures, none of which were adequate, some of which were downright painful. Eighteenth-century dentistry was about as ineffectual as eighteenth-century medicine. "His Excellency" had kept his figure, weighing about 170 to 180 pounds, well proportioned to his height of about six feet, probably due as much to his moderate eating and drinking habits as to his exercise. But he felt himself to be growing old and feared he would not much longer be physically and mentally equal to the demands of his office.

And those demands were about to increase substantially. Secretary Hamilton had been commissioned by Congress to draft a plan for funding the debts of the old Congress. The "First Report on the

Public Credit," submitted in January 1790, was in the main unexceptionable. Hamilton proposed to pay off the old debt, estimated to total almost $80 million—foreign, congressional, and state debts included—at face value, with interest on the domestic debt to be a little more than 4 percent; whatever interest the foreign debt contracts called for would be paid. The present holders of the debt certificates were to be the new bond holders. Thus Hamilton dismissed the idea of scaling the debt down or discriminating in favor of the original holders who, in many cases, had sold their certificates for a fraction of their face value. There was sentiment in favor of both expedients, but neither was able to muster many votes in Congress. The Constitution had been put into effect partly to pay off the debt and, considering the wide range of policies from which Hamilton could choose, he had served the fiscal needs of the nation well. But the proposal, on grounds of both equity and policy, that the national government assume the debts incurred by the states in fighting the war, snapped the patience of the agrarian sectionalists who, while none too happy with the new, stronger central government, had borne with it. Paradoxically, Madison, the arch-nationalist of the 1780s, was their leader; his nationalism had put him into serious political trouble in Virginia, where he had to campaign hard for election to the First Congress; now he was fighting for his political life.[12]

Washington played no direct role in the controversy. As he was careful to say nothing while Congress was deliberating, one can make only surmises. He may have favored discrimination on ground of equity to the soldiers who had been forced to sell their pay warrants in 1783; he had certainly felt strongly about it then. In 1789 he had drafted a plan calling for the federal government to collect all taxes; he felt this would be more just and would increase the loyalty of citizens to the central government. Anything constitutional and reasonable which would increase the power of that government would be favored by Washington, so he might have approved of assumption. But the only comment he made was to regret the controversy which arose over it. To him the quarrel was sectional, not fiscal, and involved no constitutional questions. At one point he complained that his fellow Virginians were extraordinarily "irritable, sour, and discontented" about assumption, so he obviously had little patience with them.

But Washington was not so nationalistic that he had no regional attachments, and the quarrel over assumption took a turn which caused it to come out so that the needs of both the nation and the

Chesapeake area were, in his opinion, well served. In order to get assumption through Congress, Hamilton found it necessary to buy votes by locating the proposed capital somewhere on the Potomac River and changing the manner by which the accounts between the old Congress and the states were being settled, the last an item of concern to Virginia, which had paid off most of its debt but believed itself to be Congress's creditor by a large sum. These matters arranged, bills were passed providing for assumption and for a capital city to be located on the Potomac. The government would move there after a ten-year stay in Philadelphia, beginning in November 1790, to permit the government buildings to be built.

Thus the Potomac would get a city which most Southerners expected to grow into an important commercial city, served by Washington's improved Potomac River so that the city could get rich serving the growing needs of Western commerce. This was just the kind of development which the president felt was most needed in the South. None of the Jeffersonian fears of the social and political evils large cities reputedly brought with them was expressed by the master of Mount Vernon. While he could not see himself living anywhere other than Mount Vernon, he realized that to grow and prosper the nation needed more than an agrarian economy; during the New England tour he had shown much interest in the factories he had visited and he approved of discrimination in favor of American manu- factures and commerce so that they might be built up. Just as the nation needed a balanced economy, so too did the Chesapeake region. Maclay's comment that the president was the primary, though hidden, force behind the Potomac residence bill was both inaccurate and unfair, but Washington did welcome the bill.[13]

While assumption had not presented any constitutional difficulties to Washington, that was not the case with the next proposal of Hamilton. In December 1790 the House was urged to establish a national bank to serve as the government's fiscal agent but also to bring the benefits of a large, well-funded bank to the private economy. The Bank of the United States was to have a capital of $10 million, 20 percent of which would be paid in by the government, which would also share in the bank's governance to that extent. A portion of the capital would consist of government bonds and its charter would last as long as the bonds were outstanding. No one except a few diehard agrarians were against banks in general or even this bank in particular. The difficulty lay with the federal govern- ment's power to establish it. A proposal to permit the government to issue charters of incorporation had been voted down at the Philadelphia Convention, and even while the Congress debated the bank bill, the Tenth Amendment—specifying what all had understood to be the case, that any power not expressly delegated by the Constitution, was reserved to the states or the people—was being ratified. The constitutional question was not strongly debated in Congress where the only change the bank bill incurred was a twenty-year term to its charter.[14]

Washington received the bill on February 16, 1791, and now had ten days to sign it or it would become law without his signature. He had already questioned the Cabinet separately on the point and both Randolph and Jefferson had criticized the bank on the grounds that the power to incorporate was not expressly delegated. Knox simply agreed with Hamilton, who was now given his adversaries' statements and instructed to answer the constitutional objections. The Treasury secretary came back on the twenty-third with a 15,000-word defense of the bank's constitutionality which relied on a liberal interpretation of the clause granting Congress authority "to make all Laws necessary and proper for carrying into execution all the foregoing Powers" [Art. I, Sec. 8]. Hamilton argued that "necessary" included all means convenient and not ruled out by either the Constitution or morality. The paper demonstrated the kind of development which the Constitution would have to undergo if it were to be an adequate instrument of government for an expanding and changing country. Jefferson and Madison opposed the bill not only because of the constitutional question but also because they had come to distrust Hamilton's objectives, believing that he wished to distort the Constitution into a virtually unlimited grant of power to a government modeled as much as circumstances permitted on England's. For the moment, their objections were focused on the claimed unconstitutionality of the proposal.

What the effect of this debate was on Washington is hard to say. After reading Hamilton's brilliant defense, he signed the bill, but this did not mean he was convinced of the bill's constitutionality. He may have been following Jefferson's advice to sign out of respect for Congress's judgment if his own mind was still undecided. Or the deciding factor may have been Washington's desire to see a government worthy of the name come out of the Constitution. Jefferson was proposing a base, a scope so circumscribed that the president may have been unpleasantly reminded of the old Congress. One indication that he did approve of the bank is found in his Annual Message in

1791. When it had been organized the previous July, rights—dubbed "scrip"—for stock were sold for $25; this scrip became the object of intense speculation, with prices going up as high as $325. Although this shocked Jefferson, Madison, and others, Washington approvingly mentioned it as a sign of the prosperity of the nation.

The day after the bank bill became law, Washington signed a tax bill placing excise taxes on a variety of items, chief among them "spiritous liquors of domestic manufacture," i.e., rum and whiskey. There were no constitutional questions here; rather, those that developed were political. Sectional interests had been upset, then accommodated in the assumption controversy, but with the bank and the excise there had been no accommodation. The opponents of these measures were clustered in the South, and as early as March 1790 Washington had been warned by David Stuart that his home state felt alone and friendless against a "Northern phalanx . . . so firmly united as to bear down all opposition." Washington's reply reproved the South, Virginia especially, for not seeing and steadily pursuing their real interests; if the North had more votes, the South would have to accept it until they could do better. Disunionist talk, such as Stuart had relayed, undermined the basis of the Union, mutual accommodation. Washington would have to repeat this again and again as he tried to deal with the effects of fast-increasing party feeling on his administration. As he saw it, the future belonged to the United States; all they had to do was stay together and let the development of half a continent carry them to greatness. There was much that was flexible in the future and opposition to a specific measure of the administration did not indicate disloyalty to the government, nor could one or several bills undermine the Constitution.

But Madison and Jefferson could not bear with the direction of public affairs as they were afraid the country would not remain a republic long enough to realize its glorious future. Years later Jefferson recorded his dismay at the preference for monarchy he found among people within and without the government when he arrived in New York in 1790; he also believed that Hamilton's fiscal system was designed first to confuse the people, and then to enrich the legislators. Seeing the country galloping into monarchy, Madison in Congress and Jefferson in the executive branch began to oppose as well as they could the policies they saw as warping the Constitution into a near grant of absolute power which could end only with the duplication in America of the corrupt and unrepresentative government of England. Neither believed Washington was helping this along. "Unversed in financial projects and calculations and budgets, his approbation of [Hamilton's policies] was bottomed on his confidence" in the man, Jefferson observed.[15] The president not only retained confidence in both secretaries but he also refused, at first, to be disheartened at opposition in the Congress. When the First Congress adjourned in March 1791, he blithely observed to Humphreys, now minister to Portugal, that "our public credit is restored, our resources are increasing, and the general appearance of things at least equals the most sanguine expectation that was formed of the effects of the present government." Although "great harmony and cordiality" prevailed throughout Congress, Washington admitted to Humphreys that, on the bank and the excise, "the line between the southern and eastern interests appeared more strongly marked than could have been wished. . . . But the debates were conducted with temper and candor." Few Congressmen would have subscribed to so rosy a view of affairs.

Nor would Washington, if he had been thinking of his private affairs. His nephew George Augustine had been a satisfactory steward; the young man had recently married and seemed settled for the foreseeable future at Mount Vernon. But when Washington visited there in the fall of 1791 he found the estate suffering from the combined effects of a drought and his nephew's serious illness. Just as the president had whipped things back into shape, he had to return unexpectedly to Philadelphia. The return was unexpected only because he had absentmindedly set the Congress's convening back one week later than it was actually scheduled for. With a good bit of self-reproach for his poor memory, he sent off a flurry of instructions to the secretaries about his message to Congress and, leaving the estate in the hands of his head farmer, Anthony Whiting, a recent emigrant from England, he himself left for the capital.

Despite Washington's concern about his speech to Congress, it proved, when it was delivered on October 25, to be mainly a list of items previously recommended to the Congress but not yet acted upon. He did express hope that the "misconception" over the excise tax held in certain parts of the country would soon be corrected and advised the Congress to deal promptly with any legitimate grievances which were discovered. They were also informed of the selection of a site on the Potomac for the new capital and were given an optimistic report on its progress.

This almost casual reference to the new capital probably concealed a good bit of satisfaction on Washington's part. From the passage of the residence bill on, the president took a great interest in the progress of the federal city. He selected a site at the junction of the Eastern Branch and the Potomac, at the southern edge of the area marked out by Congress. In the 1780s, when the old Congress had thought about a permanent home for itself, a site near Washington's choice had been tentatively selected so the area had been marked out already as a suitable location for a capital. The small commercial towns of Georgetown and Alexandria, included within the ten-mile square ceded by Maryland and Virginia, were looked to as nuclei for the commercial center the capital was expected to become. In 1791 the name "Washington" was selected for the city and "District of Columbia" for the entire square, and commissioners were appointed to purchase land, lay out streets, supervise the construction of the federal buildings, etc. Although the commissioners frequently conferred with the president and seem never to have done anything he disagreed with, their appointment removed from his shoulders the primary responsibility for the work. He followed its progress eagerly, always visiting the city when he was staying at Mount Vernon. As late as February 1792 he was sufficiently nervous about the continuing opposition to removing the government from Philadelphia to worry that any slowdown resulting from the discharge of the project's superintendent, Pierre L'Enfant, would be a "deathblow." Senator Maclay had been wrong in 1790 when he believed Washington to be the chief mover of a southern capital, but if he had written those lines a year or two later, he would have been close to the truth.[16]

The Congress took up the president's shopping list and began to act on it in desultory fashion while he fretted over the news from Mount Vernon. His nephew continued to decline, but Whiting was showing surprising competence. The situation was similarly mixed in Philadelphia; George Hammond presented himself to the president in November as the first English minister to the United States, but the next month brought notice of the defeat of an American force under Major-General Arthur St. Clair by the Indians of the Northwest. England, still in possession of posts on American soil, might have sent a minister but would they negotiate in the face of American weakness? St. Clair's defeat also led to a congressional investigation, the first of its kind. A request from the House for executive papers pertaining to the expedition was complied with, although it was realized that this could present difficulties in the future. The investigation exonerated both St. Clair and the administration and actually helped to build up support for a stronger force.

But the Second Congress did give the president a serious dilemma. In reapportioning the House according to the findings of the First Census, each state was given one representative for each 30,000 unit of its population. So far, it was a simple exercise in division. But the remaining population was then thrown into one national pot and representatives were dealt out, with a good deal of horse trading, to the various states. In the process, not only was the South seriously shortchanged but states were represented according to different ratios. For this reason Jefferson and Randolph advised the president to veto the bill; Hamilton and Knox argued that, since the Constitution was not clear and Congress's interpretation was a reasonable one, it should be accepted. Washington delayed because the bill had become a sectional issue and he did not want to appear to favor his own section. But Jefferson argued that a desire to avoid the appearance of favoritism should not induce the president to do wrong. Convinced, he asked Jefferson, Randolph, and Madison, who had also been consulted, to draft a veto message, which was delivered to Congress on April 5, 1792. Just nine days later a bill applying a uniform ratio of 33,000 inhabitants per representative to each state was given to Washington for his signature. This quick action by Congress showed their ready agreement with the first exercise of the executive veto.

While Congress was computing its electoral arithmetic, Washington was doing some counting of his own. He had celebrated his sixtieth birthday in February, marking sixteen years of his adult life spent in public service, first for the king, then for the Republic. He certainly deserved retirement. He was also concerned about his reputation; as he told Jefferson, accepting a second term "might give room to say, that having tasted the sweets of office, he could not do without them." What he saw as the effects of old age on his health and memory also bothered him and, with his inability to exercise, his office was "more irksome, and tranquility and retirement become an irresistible passion." He seemed determined not to accept election to a second term.[17]

Confirming and strengthening Washington's decision to retire was the quarreling of his Secretaries at the more-frequent Cabinet meetings now being called to save some of the time used in individual consultation. These quarrels were duplicated in Congress and in newspapers which quickly developed partisan attachments to either the opposition "Republicans," as they had begun to call themselves, or those who supported Hamilton's policies, the "Federalists." Washington did his best to stay aloof from these contentions, partly from personal preference, partly because he did not believe his office permitted partisan activity. But the Republican attacks on Hamilton's fiscal system began to tell on the president also and he complained to Jefferson in July that "in condemning the administration of government, they condemned him, for if there were measures pursued contrary to his sentiments, they must conceive him too careless to attend to them, or too stupid to understand them." He was especially critical of the *National Gazette,* whose editor, Philip Freneau, also worked as a part-time translator in the State Department. The *Gazette,* Washington felt, was trying to promote disunion by exciting opposition to the government and, if Jefferson really feared monarchy, what would be more likely to bring it on than the chaos caused by the breakup of the Union? Jefferson replied by repeating his criticism of the funding system for corrupting the legislature and milking the South in order to pay off the bonds held by the North, among other evils.[18]

Jefferson's charges, however, sufficiently upset Washington that he rephrased them and, in August, asked Hamilton to answer them. The Treasury secretary conceded nothing other than that some might have been hurt by speculating in government bonds but he saw no way of preventing that. To the charge that he was promoting monarchy, the secretary gave the same answer which Washington had already given, that the easiest way to do this was to promote instability and the easiest way to that was to "resist a confirmation of public order." Washington tried to reconcile his two aides with almost identical letters to each in which he pleaded that "instead of wounding suspicions and irritable charges, there may be liberal allowances, mutual forebearances and temporizing yieldings on *all sides* [orig. emph.]." In replying, Hamilton did concede that he had helped with the recent attacks on Jefferson in the Federalist press but he defended this as mere self-defense against charges which Freneau, Jefferson's minion, was daily leveling against him. Jefferson simply repeated his charges, including Hamilton's interference in State Department affairs (true), and denied that he had any share in Freneau's writing (technically true). He concluded by stating his intention to retire in March 1793. Despite obviously half-hearted promises by each secretary to keep the peace in the Cabinet, Washington could see that the two men disliked and distrusted each other intensely and were not soon likely to change their minds.[19]

Paradoxically, this evidence of personal and partisan discontent, reflecting as it did sectional discontent, was probably helping to change Washington's mind about retiring. It underlined the point Jefferson made in June: "The confidence of the whole union is centered in you . . . North & South will hang together, if they have you to hang on." Everyone Washington talked with concurred in this—Hamilton, Madison, Lear. The last had occasion to go to New England during the summer and reported that all there wanted the president to continue. The need for union was self-evident to Washington; in May when directing Madison in the drafting of his valedictory, he told him to stress the common bonds uniting the country: "that we are *all* [orig. emph.] the children of the same country," and the interests of all Americans were the same; the economic interests of all sections could be made to march together to the mutual enrichment of all. These are truisms and they are more valuable for what they show of Washington's concerns than for the advice they contain. For he was also worried about the harsh criticism of public officials in the press; "there ought to be limits to it; for suspicions unfounded, and jealousies too lively, are irritating to honest feelings." Thus on the one hand he was being told that all believed him to be the hinge on which the Union turned, but on the other hand his agents and the policies of his administration were being severely criticized, and he was certainly the "indirect object" of some of this criticism. As ever, the currents seemed contradictory and confusing, not a clear guide at all.

While preparing for what he hoped would be his last speech to the Congress, Washington also had to worry over objections to the excise that were surfacing in some sections, especially western Pennsylvania. An executive proclamation warning all citizens to refrain from opposition to the law was sent out, but the President feared that more stringent measures, perhaps even troops, would be necessary before matters quieted down. This was just the kind of trouble, his advisors assured him, which only his presence kept from flaring up into something more serious. His Annual Message, delivered to Congress on November 6, referred to the complaints of the Pennsylvanians but only to assure the legislators that the laws would be enforced. The Message concerned mainly Indian policy, detailing the steps taken to defend the frontier but also pleading for congressional support for a more just and humane policy toward the natives. His statements here were an interesting contrast to those he had made as Colonel of the Virginia Regiment when the Indians were seen only as malignant obstacles to Virginia's progress westward. Despite his resentment over the newspaper attacks on the administration, he also asked Congress to consider whether or not postal rates were discouraging their circulation; he was ready to criticize the press but he was not ready to do without it.

The last time Washington had had to make a fateful decision was in 1789; then it had been impossible to say at what point he had decided to accept the presidency. Similarly, in 1792, he said nothing and did nothing and by that means slowly but inextricably slid into his second term. As late as November 4 a close friend of the president's was not certain he had decided to stay on. But the Electoral College met on schedule the first Monday in December, and from that point on Washington was going to serve another term, the prospect of his declining it after election being inconceivable.

One thing helped to make Washington's election to a second term a pleasant event; as the votes were made known in early January, it was seen that no one had voted against him. In urging him to stand for election, Hamilton had derided the idea that anyone would vote against him, so apparently this prospect had worried the president. Negative votes would have been a kind of confirmation of his fears that his presence had become a disuniting force. Vice-President Adams received seventy-seven votes, the remaining fifty going to George Clinton in a half-hearted Republican attempt to unseat the man who was wrongly credited by some with trying to push monarchy onto the American people. Except for the gratifying unanimity of his reelection, however, little else promised that Washington's second term would be either easy or tranquil.

In February 1793 Washington secured from his Secretary of State a promise to stay until the end of the year, although he would not promise to try to get along with Hamilton. Jefferson protested that *he* had never conspired against a colleague and, if Virginia was restless, as Washington had heard from Henry Lee, it was only because of the constant losses southern interests suffered at the hands of the stock jobbers in Congress. This wrung from Washington the almost anguished cry that, while everyone was urging him to remain, few realized "the extreme wretchedness of his existence while in office." Just a few weeks later, as he celebrated his sixty-first birthday, he learned of the death of his nephew George Augustine; in addition to the loss of a dearly loved relative, Washington now had to secure a new estate manager. Whiting, already acting in that capacity, would have to do for the time being. Washington directed him by means of long letters written every Sunday morning; they were incredibly detailed and showed, in addition to his intimate knowledge of his farms, that his memory, at least as far as Mount Vernon was concerned, was as good as ever.[20]

In assessing his first term, Washington may well have judged it to be rather close to what he expected it to be, a mixed blessing. The administrative and social chores of the office had been burdensome, the realization that he was helping the new nation through a difficult adolescence a more than adequate compensation. But the major difficulties he had experienced were completely unexpected; the party animosities in Congress and their spread into his official family seemed to him useless demonstrations of an incomprehensible fear of the legitimate operations of the new government. To Washington, experience was the best and only teacher; Americans must be willing to trust the Constitution and its government not to stray beyond the bounds marked out for it. What he feared most was anarchy, the sad state from which he believed the Constitution had saved the country in 1789.

The primary task of the new president had been twofold: to get the new government functioning and to plant it firmly in the affections of the people. Washington had clearly succeeded in the first and, if the discord in Cabinet and Congress plus the newspaper war was any indication, partially failed in the second. This partial failure should not be allowed to obscure the substantial success achieved. The government had been organized and was working efficiently and effectively; the office of the president had been satisfactorily executed along the lines of the narrow conception of the office held by Washington and most of his successors. If the new government could enjoy a few more years of tranquility, perhaps the difficulties foreseen by the Republicans would disappear as the strength of the United States translated itself into increasing prosperity and freedom for its citizens. An America isolated from the consuming furies of Europe which had been set free by the French Revolution might have had that tranquility. But Washington's America was not isolated.

CHAPTER 6

The Task Completed? 1793–1797

What with the current affairs of the government, the unpleasant aspect of matters on our Indian frontiers, and the momentous occurrences in Europe, I am not only pressed with the quantity of business but the nature of a great part of it is particularly delicate and embarassing.

AS a kind of sign of the division already affecting the country, the Cabinet could not agree on the ceremonial details of Washington's second inauguration. The president followed Randolph and Knox's advice and took his oath before both houses in a brief, almost commonplace ceremony in the Senate chamber. Before taking the oath he stated that he would "express the high sense I entertain of this distinguished honor" at a later date, for now he was content to note

that if it shall be found during my administration of the government I have in any instance violated willingly or knowingly the injunction thereof, I may (besides incurring Constitutional punishment) be subject to the upbraidings of all who are now witnesses of the present solemn ceremony.

It was a curious statement for such an occasion and, whatever else it might indicate, it certainly showed that the sense of adventure and imminent high accomplishment of 1789 had evaporated amidst the division in the Cabinet, the opposition in Congress, and the partisan contention in the country at large. Originating in disagreement over Hamilton's fiscal system, it had been exacerbated by a disagreement among Americans over the aims and measures of the French Revolution. At its start, most Americans wished well to the country which had so materially aided theirs in its struggle for independence. But, among those who knew France well, there were early doubts that this revolution would proceed smoothly. Washington contented himself with cordial but vague replies when French correspondents informed him of conditions there. "Of one thing, however, you may rest perfectly assured, that nobody is more anxious for the happy

109

issue of that business than I am, as nobody can wish more sincerely for the prosperity of the French Nation, than I do," he assured the Chevalier la Luzerne in April 1790. As the Revolution progressed, both the hopes and fears of Americans were confirmed, more or less in agreement with the original positions taken, for its progress was sufficiently complicated to permit anyone to take comfort or alarm. A fondness for France and a willingness to believe that somehow things there would work out seemed to accompany an antipathy for Hamilton's fiscal system and for England. Other issues developed, but these remained primary: finances and the country's relations with England and France. These were the issues that divided the pro-English Federalists from the pro-French Republicans, the "Anglo-men" from the "Gallomen," the "monocrats" or "paper men" from the "democrats" or "Jacobins," to use some of their favorite pejoratives for each other. Actually Hamilton's supporters were more or less bound to a pro-English attitude for their mentor's system, relying as it did on a high volume of trade for a steady flow of revenue from the tariff, trade in which, independent or not, England remained the republic's major partner. Once England joined the alliance of monarchs fighting to contain the revolution, she could also be supported as one of the chief fighters for a proper concept of liberty and order. But this gave the Republicans yet another reason for disliking the English.[1]

Washington managed to remain aloof from these developing party tensions during his first term, especially as they translated themselves into a preference for either England or France. This was not easy as each of these powers, plus Spain, retained a lively interest in North America. A 1790 war scare between England and Spain, the Nootka Sound Controversy, touched off a Cabinet discussion on a response to any attempt by England to move troops across the American west to attack the Spanish in the lower Mississippi Valley. Besides illustrating the powerlessness of the country, the discussion also showed Washington's anti-English disposition; for, although he realized that all the United States could do is protest, he wanted the protest to be in the strongest possible language. But these feelings did not influence his conception of a proper policy; as he confided to Lafayette in July

Gradually recovering from the distresses in which the war left us, patiently advancing in our task of civil government, unentangled in the crooked politics of Europe, wanting scarcely any thing but the free navigation of the

Mississippi (which we must have and as certainly shall have as we remain a nation) I have supposed, that, with the undeviating exercise of a just, steady, and prudent national policy, we shall be the gainers, whether the powers of the old world may be in peace or war, but more especially in the latter case. In that case, our importance will certainly increase, and our friendship be courted.

To paraphrase the cliché much loved by diplomatic historians: Europe's distresses just might be America's successes.[2]

The pursuance of a "just, steady, and prudent national policy" was no easy thing, however. The English retained seven military posts in the United States, on the presumed ground of American nonfulfillment of the 1783 treaty; actually the posts aided them in their dominance of the fur trade. Washington was convinced that their presence, especially in the Northwest, encouraged the Indians there in their intermittent warfare against American settlers. Another difficulty, previously noted, was the commercial discrimination England practiced against the United States. Nothing having been accomplished in any of these areas, Washington looked forward to the coming of an English minister, but Hammond lacked instructions on any of the topics that upset the United States.

In the Mississippi Valley, Spain's control of New Orleans blocked the easiest route for American goods from the West; the Spanish were also suspected of inciting the Indians in the Southwest. Indeed the Valley was a kind of focus for the American policies of all three Atlantic powers; each wished to keep the United States east of the Appalachians. But for Washington, as for most Americans, the West was the surety that the United States would one day, and that day not far in the future, be a great power. In a sense, the European war brought on by the revolution postponed any vigorous action by England or France (Spain was capable of no more than a holding action) to realize their Mississippi dreams until the United States had a firm hold in the West. Although the long-term effects of the wars of the French Revolution and Napoleon may have been beneficial for the United States, in the short run they were anything but that, as Washington discovered in April 1793.

When Washington left for Mount Vernon late in March, he knew of Louis XVI's execution and the declaration of a republic. Edmond Charles Genet (later famous, or infamous, as your historical politics may dictate, as "Citizen Genet") was already on the way to his post as Minister to the United States. Should he arrive in Washington's absence, Jefferson was directed to receive him correctly but with no undue cordiality. In Virginia Washington busied himself with Mount Vernon's tangled affairs and the funeral of his nephew while the news from Europe remained vague, with Jefferson disparaging rumors of a general war in Europe involving England as the garbled reports of the new republic's condemnations of monarchy, statements of philosophy, nothing more.[3] The president hoped Jefferson was right, but for the moment he was more interested in why the governor and judge of the Northwest Territory were still in Philadelphia and not at their posts; the government was not going to stop because of events 3,000 miles away. Hamilton was the first to advise the president that reliable reports of a European war, involving England, had come to the capital. Washington replied that he would return as soon as possible; until then the secretaries should ponder how to keep the United States neutral. "A strict neutrality" would be needed to keep individuals from involving the country with either of the principal—to the United States—belligerents, England and France.

Reaching Philadelphia on April 17, Washington plunged into the work of evaluating the war's effect on American policy. As he did so, he discovered that his Secretary of State had only a few general thoughts on a proper policy for a neutral. Quite the contrary with Hamilton, who presented the president with a list of questions regarding our conduct toward France and the validity of the 1778 treaties with her. Lacking any other advice, Washington used the list almost verbatim as an agenda for a Cabinet meeting on the morning of the nineteenth. Although Jefferson resented his colleague's role, he had only himself to blame; the Secretary of the Treasury had done his homework; the Secretary of State had not.[4]

The meeting was able to settle only two of the thirteen questions Hamilton had posed. Despite Jefferson's objections, it was decided to issue an official statement of policy. The Secretary of State believed this to be possibly unconstitutional and imprudent, unconstitutional because only the Congress had the power to declare war—could the president unilaterally declare neutrality or no war?—imprudent because Jefferson hoped that perhaps England might bid for neutrality with a liberal policy toward American shipping. The president and his other advisors saw only peril, not opportunity, in silence. With a nod to Jefferson's sensibilities by directing that the word "neutrality" not be used, Washington commissioned Randolph to draft the proclamation. The attorney-general was becoming more significant in the president's circle of advisors, partly as a result of the partisan squabbling of Jefferson and Hamilton. Cursed with an ability to see both sides, Randolph had cast the deciding vote on a number of significant issues; because Jefferson could not be certain how he would go, he had become resentful and styled his colleague a "chameleon." Chameleon or no, Randolph had supported Jefferson more than Hamilton and had earned the president's gratitude for often giving him a middle ground between the extremes of Treasury and State. Faced with Knox's literary incapacity, Washington naturally turned to the only available person who could draft an announcement without its becoming the object of interminable wrangling. More such work would be Randolph's lot in the future.[5]

The second question, whether or not a new French minister should be received, had already been answered when Washington had directed the American minister to Paris, Gouverneur Morris, to extend recognition to the Republic. Next the Cabinet was asked whether the minister should be received unconditionally. Here Hamilton was implicitly questioning the validity of the 1778 treaties now that France was a republic, not a monarchy. Jefferson countered, with Randolph's support, that treaties were made with nations, not governments, and could not be affected by the death of a king. When Hamilton supported his stand with a quotation from Vattel, the writer on international law, and Jefferson challenged its relevance, Randolph took advantage of the disagreement to suggest an adjournment so the authority could be consulted. Washington probably appreciated Randolph's tact in postponing, possibly preventing, another squabble between Hamilton and Jefferson; another meeting was called for the following Monday, April twenty-second.

But by that time Randolph had a draft of the policy statement ready, so the meeting was spent going over it instead of Vattel. The statement advised all nations that the United States would "pursue a conduct friendly and impartial toward the belligerent Powers"; despite the avoidance of the word "neutrality," it quickly became known as the "Neutrality Proclamation." Within a week Jefferson had, in a report to Washington, refuted Hamilton's aspersions on the validity of the treaties, even showing where his colleague had misconstrued Vattel, and there was no further discussion on that score. There was a good bit more talk, however, on how the United States could live up to its obligations as a neutral. The problem was, given the limited number of federal officials and the political unreliability of some state and local officers, how a rule forbidding the fitting out of privateers in American ports could be enforced.

Randolph suggested using customs collectors, but only as useful adjuncts to federal attorneys. Jefferson resented the use of any Treasury Department officials, but he did not realize that this was a Washington-Randolph modification of a plan suggested by Hamilton which would have used customs collectors only. While partisanship was lessening the effectiveness of Jefferson, independence was increasing the value of Randolph.

Enforcement of American neutrality regulations was one of the most difficult tasks the administration confronted. Already the English minister, Hammond, had complained about the fitting out of several French privateers in southern ports. These complaints reminded Washington that, although he had landed in Charleston in early April, the French minister had not yet appeared in Philadelphia. At length, on May 16, Genet made a triumphal entrance, welcomed enthusiastically by local Republicans and a salute from a visiting French warship. Accompanied by Jefferson, he presented his credentials to the president on the eighteenth. Few details of the occasion survive, but apparently Washington, as he frequently did, contented himself with as few words as possible, thus putting off the voluble Frenchman; he had long since discovered that silence had its uses. Genet had expected to find in America a sympathetic partner in the struggle against monarchical government which all right-thinking people would presently join. When he found instead an administration intent on keeping him at arm's length, he made the mistake of assuming popular support for the policy and tried to communicate directly with the people. This was his first mistake; he did not make too many others, for his stay was too short.[6]

Jefferson's initial reaction to Genet was admiring, almost effusive; by early July the secretary considered the minister "hot headed, all imagination, no judgement, passionate, disrespectful and even indecent" toward Washington.[7] Although he kept his counsel, the president probably shared these sentiments. Genet's demands for the immediate payment of the principal of the French debt and a new alliance between the two republics could be considered and, at length, rejected; what could not be tolerated were Genet's continued violations of diplomatic protocol and, in at least one instance, bad faith. A French privateer had seized an English merchantman, the *Little Sarah*; the vessel had been condemned by a French prize court; Genet purchased it, renaming it *La Petite Democrate*, and began to fit it out as a privateer. Since Hammond was protesting the original seizure and the legality of the conversion, by American law, was questionable, Jefferson secured what he believed was a promise from Genet that the vessel would stay moored in Philadelphia for the time being.

Washington was especially ill-equipped to deal with annoying matters of this sort as he was ill with a low fever for several weeks; he erupted at Jefferson late in May about Freneau's attacks, which had previously gone unmentioned. Then he had to go to Mount Vernon in June to deal with problems created by the serious illness of Whiting; when he arrived there, he found the steward dead, and with no replacement at hand the estate had to be left in the hands of the overseers of the five farms, unsatisfactory but the best that could be done when he left in early July. Reaching Philadelphia, he discovered that Genet had put the *Democrate* down the Delaware, beyond the reach of the authorities. Jefferson was quizzed sharply as to why the president had not been informed of this earlier; then he was asked,

Is the Minister of the French Republic to set the acts of this Government at defiance with impunity? And then threaten the Executive with an appeal to the people? What must the world think of such conduct, and of the Government of the U[nited]. States for submitting to it?

By the end of the month, the Cabinet had agreed that Genet's recall had to be requested and "Rules Concerning Belligerents" had been drawn up and published. Now no one could take refuge by charging vagueness on the part of the Administration. But Washington's temper continued high and, at an early August meeting considering whether or not to publish Genet's correspondence, he lost it altogether, according to Jefferson.

The President was much inflamed; got into one of those passions when he cannot command himself; ran on much on the personal abuse which had been bestowed on him; defied any man on earth to produce one single act of his since he had been in the government, which was not done on the purest motives; that he had never repented but once the having slipped the moment of resigning his office, and that was every moment since; that *by God* he had rather be in his grave than in his present situation; that he had rather be on his farm than to be made *Emperor of the world*; and yet they were charging him with wanting to be a King. That that *rascal Freneau* sent him three of his papers every day, as if he thought he would become the distributor of his papers; that he could see in this, nothing but an impudent design to insult him [orig. emph.].[8]

Although his anger at Freneau was directed in part at Jefferson also, a few days later Washington talked the secretary into staying for the rest of the year; thus even as the partisan contention deepened, the president tried to keep the Cabinet, if not nonpartisan, at least bipartisan. But he himself was slipping from that standard. While he had been unsparing in his denunciation of Freneau, nothing was said to Hamilton about his "No Jacobin" essays, answers to "Jacobin's" defense of Genet, which had appeared in July.

All this was cut short by an entirely nonpartisan phenomenon which appeared in Philadelphia in August, yellow fever. Under the pressure of an epidemic which saw deaths reaching 100 a day by early October, government and most other organized activities almost disappeared. Washington was alarmed for the safety of his family, but Martha refused to be sent away. In order not to dispirit the people, he waited until the normal date for his fall visit to Mount Vernon, September 10, before leaving.

About this time Washington began to connect Genet's activities, which disturbed him even at Mount Vernon, with those of the Democratic-Republican Societies, political groups which had originated coincidentally with Genet's arrival, although they had no direct, causative connection with the emissary. Beginning with the Democratic Society of Pennsylvania in Philadelphia, organized in July 1793, the clubs spread throughout the country; they held political discussions, sent out propaganda, and generally espoused, in any way they could, the cause of the French Revolution. Although they were not part of the Republican party, often the same people were active in both and the societies frequently worked for Republican candidates. But Washington did not view them at all dispassionately and confided to Henry Lee, Governor of Virginia, that their purpose was "nothing short of the subversion of the Government of these States, even at the expense of plunging this country in the horrors of a disastrous war." For now, he did not link the societies directly with France but rather lumped them with those trying to involve the country in a war, which group did include the French minister.[9]

With the arrival of cold weather, the fever abated in the capital and, by the time Congress was scheduled to convene, life was nearly normal in the city, but the losses had been heavy. Washington's fifth Annual Address was delivered on December 3. His explanation of the Neutrality Proclamation was plain and straightforward: "It seemed . . . my duty" because "our disposition for peace" might be questioned by the belligerents if they saw Americans participating in contraband trade or hostile acts. After briefly explaining the rules regarding belligerents, he handed the topic on to Congress to deal with as they saw fit. Separate messages would be sent later dealing with our relations with England, France, Spain, and the Barbary states. Otherwise the message noted some difficulties with the Indians and recommended close attention to defense. The special messages followed soon after and, in the case of France, detailed Genet's conduct as a justification for his recall. England's non-compliance with the Treaty of 1783, especially in the matter of the military posts and her bland refusal to negotiate seriously any of the outstanding difficulties, was explained. This message was a minor triumph for Jefferson, who had countered Hamilton's strong arguments that the English minister's correspondence should not be published. Washington had insisted, against a majority of the Cabinet, that both records, the French and English, be given to Congress (and through them to the people) as justification for the steps that had been taken. On the sixteenth, as a kind of valedictory, Jefferson submitted a report, requested by Congress, on discrimination against American commerce by its major foreign customers and suppliers; it showed that England was the major offender on this score and called for retaliatory action by the Congress. At the end of the year Jefferson resigned and was replaced by Randolph. In a graceful letter, Washington acknowledged his ex-secretary's work and commented that it showed the correctness of his initial appointment.

The easy replacement of Jefferson with Randolph gratified the president, whose mind was also made easier by the hiring of a competent manager, William Pearce, for Mount Vernon. As 1794 began, most of the major problems confronting the administration seemed to be under control and Washington might have expected a quiet period for the immediate future. Certainly Genet would no longer plague the government; the State Department learned on January 20 that a replacement was on the way. And the House began, but then postponed until March, consideration of Jefferson's report on commercial discrimination. But the signs predicting a quiet time were misleading.

Before the end of February Washington learned of extensive ship seizures in the West Indies; apparently England was determined to cut off trade between the United States and the French islands. To compound the injury, some of the crews were being impressed while their ships were detained. Even the promulgation of an order forbidding neutral trade with the French was insulting; instead of a warning period, it went into effect on the day it was announced in London so that some vessels were seized which had left port when no one outside the Foreign Ministry and the Admiralty could have known that their voyages might be illegal. Congress's response was thundering and, for once, bipartisan; a thirty-day embargo was passed and went into effect on March 28. Adding to the legislators' agitation was the report of a speech by Lord Dorchester, Governor-General of Canada, to some Indians assuring them of English aid in the event of an expected war between them and the United States. Now, just at the wrong time, resolutions based on Jefferson's December 1793 report came up for House debate. They found an excited and agreeable audience. Despite the prompt English withdrawal of the West Indian order (even before American protests reached London), a bill extending the embargo until the seizures had been made good and the military posts evacuated passed the House and failed in the Senate only by John Adams's tie-breaking vote. Discriminatory tariffs and the sequestration of balances owing to English merchants were also spoken of in and out of Congress. The construction of four frigates was provided for, and coastal defenses were to be strengthened.

In the spring of 1794 the nation was in the grip of war fever because of England's repeated and blatant insults to American sovereignty and interests. Washington kept his counsel in the midst of the excitement. Early in March a Federalist senator, Oliver Ellsworth of Connecticut, suggested a special mission to England to secure a settlement and prevent war, but the suggested emissary was Hamilton; Washington frostily told the senator that his Secretary of the Treasury was not trusted by the people. The Federalists repeated the offer of Hamilton, but to no effect. Hearing of the suggestion, Senator James Monroe of Virginia, not knowing Washington's reaction, gratuitously told the president that the appointment would be as bad for Washington as for the country. This got the frosty reply that, as the appointing power was the president's, he and no one else would consider carefully whom to appoint. Washington's coolness was bipartisan. But the situation was still hot enough to merit the serious consideration of a special mission. Surveying the field, Washington could see no qualified person who was then free to take the mission. Rioting in Philadelphia, not the first instance of violence coming from the tense situation, underlined the necessity that something be done.

John Jay was, of all those mentioned to Washington, in the best position to go to England, being in the relatively undemanding position of Chief Justice. Ignoring Washington's rather pointed suggestion that he resign his seat, Jay accepted the offer of the special mission to London in mid-April. In formulating Jay's instructions, Randolph lost out to his Treasury colleague, who responded first and in detail to the president's request for help. On the surface, the instructions were quite rigorous. Jay was to obtain compensation for seized vessels and a more liberal treatment for American ships, evacuation of the military posts, and payment for slaves taken away at the end of the War; but these were desirable goals only. All that Jay was required to secure was limited entry for American vessels to the British West Indies; also, he was not to violate any treaty obligations to France. Randolph also lost in deciding whether or not Jay should sign a treaty or simply a preliminary agreement. The Secretary of State feared that Jay, in the absence of express stipulations, would let the English walk away with the negotiations. Hamilton, much more than Randolph, had set the tone and scope of the mission. In mid-May, to the sound of jeers by suspicious Republicans, Jay left for London.[10]

Now that relations with England had been put beyond the reach of the angry opposition in the House, French affairs needed looking after. The French had willingly recalled Genet but they had also requested that the United States replace Gouverneur Morris, whose obvious sympathy with the monarchists had been made harder to bear by his too-ready wit and sarcasm. (Washington had feared just this in 1792.) Getting a new envoy was no easy job. Robert R. Livingston had to decline the post twice before Washington stopped trying to recruit him. Then, apparently working on the principle that, since England had gotten an Anglophile minister plenipotentiary, France deserved a Francophile minister, the president turned closer to home and asked his fellow Virginian James Monroe to go to Paris. Monroe, disillusioned with what he thought was the decrepit state of the Republican bloc in the Senate, accepted. His confirmation was almost the last business considered by the upper house before Congress adjourned a long, bitter, and exhausting session early in June.

Congress would now have a respite from its labors, but the president and his Cabinet soon had a new threat to the peace of the country to contend with. Since 1791, the excise tax on "spiritous liquors of domestic manufacture" had been a grievance of the citizens of trans-Appalachia, who shared the historic English resentment of it as a "hateful tax levied upon commodities, and adjudged not by the common judges of property, but by wretches hired by those to whom it is paid." But they also had practical, immediate reasons for resenting certain features of the tax which, because of their unusual situation, made it especially burdensome: the levy had to be paid in cash on the produce of all stills, and all indictments under the law were to be tried in the nearest federal court. In the West many farmers did not sell their whiskey, the only way to convert a bulky crop into an easily moved commodity, but bartered it to a storeowner for necessities, paid debts, and supplemented the wages of extra hands hired for the harvest with it. Thus the farmer/distiller frequently received cash for little, if any, of his whiskey; how was he to pay the excise man with cash if he handled most of his affairs without it? And if he did not pay the excise man, he would be tried in the nearest federal court, but in the case of the center of the discontent, western Pennsylvania, that court was in Philadelphia, 300 miles and several weeks across the mountains. Further, the law exacerbated feelings endemic in the West, feelings that the law and its minions, courts, attorneys, constables, and the like were there only to trap the poor farmer in their snares and rob him of his land; anything which seemed likely to entangle him with the law was certain to be resented. Thus Hamilton's excise law would have to be carefully explained and judiciously enforced if the West, especially western Pennsylvania, was to accept it.[11]

Washington, who was no friend to tax collectors, either (he had recently styled Fairfax County's as "among the greatest rascals in the world"), was not sympathetic to the Westerners, however. They were represented in the Congress which had drawn up the legislation they were protesting so vehemently. Petitions to their representatives or directly to the president were the proper channel for presenting grievances. In 1792 Hamilton had wanted to suppress forcibly protests against the law but no one had supported him then; in 1794, new trouble sprang up partly because of Hamilton's obtuseness. Despite a recent revision of the law which permitted trial in convenient state courts, the Treasury Secretary had warrants returnable in federal court in Philadelphia sworn out because the offenses had been committed before the law was revised. When the warrant servers were forcibly resisted and an attack was made on the home of an official of the excise near Pittsburgh, an attack in which a life was lost and the home was burnt to the ground, it was obvious that the disturbances were much more than the usual grumbling. As early as April, Washington had labeled the Westerners' protests as "the first fruits of the Democratic Society" and saw Genet as their originator. Consequently he was in no mood for conciliation and compromise when news of the trouble mentioned above came to him in July. It was soon seen that force might have to be used to suppress resistance to the law. But several details had to be considered before force could be employed: where was it to be found and how was it to be authorized? Further, since the resistance centered in Pennsylvania, what actions would that state take?

Pennsylvania's authorities refused to see the trouble as beyond the reach of judicial authority and would not call out their own militia; this made the administration fearful that perhaps no state's militia would answer a federal call. James Wilson, Associate Justice of the Supreme Court, gave the necessary declaration that ordinary processes could not enforce the law, thus clearing the way for a federal summons of militia, but Randolph urged delay. News of the "rebellion" rested entirely on correspondence so far and could be exaggerated; also, troops would certainly inflame party feelings and ought to be avoided, if at all possible. And this was as it should be, for the "strength of a government is in the affections of the people," Randolph argued, and troops ought always to be the last resort. Washington had argued to much the same effect in 1792 when Hamilton had wanted to use force, so Randolph's statements probably weighed a good bit in his judgment. Instead of calling troops out precipitately, the administration now began to exhaust all other courses of action. Pennsylvania authorities were sounded out officially on August 2; they still saw no grave emergency. Next federal commissioners were sent to the troubled area with an offer of amnesty to all who would immediately stop opposing the law. This had the twin benefits of showing the conciliatory policy of the administration and of gathering firsthand information on the situation. But plans for the calling of militia continued, just in case.[12]

As the commissioners rode westward, they received conflicting reports from persons met on the road, and they sent their confusion back to Philadelphia. By the middle of September the confusion had been dispelled; it was obvious that the insurgents were at least a strong minority in the area around Pittsburgh and that they were rejecting the amnesty. Washington was now convinced that force was necessary, and he called out 12,000 men from Pennsylvania, New Jersey, Maryland, and Virginia to rendezvous at Bedford, Pennsylvania. Yet another proclamation was issued explaining the necessity of the move as Washington prepared to travel west with his secretary and Hamilton, in charge of the War Department because of Knox's absence on pressing personal business. As he left the capital, he learned of Anthony Wayne's victory over the western Indians in August at Fallen Timbers, Ohio. Now that the frontier was temporarily safe from the red savages, the white savages who refused to accept the burdens of government would have to be disciplined.

All the fears about public nonacceptance of the government's actions proved needless. The militiamen turned out and, as one marching song put it:

> To arms once more, our hero cries;
> Sedition lives and order dies.
> To peace and ease then bid adieu,
> And dash to the mountains, Jersey Blue.

They did not quite dash but they turned out willingly enough and showed themselves to be perhaps too zealous in the performance of their duties, especially in the suppression of rebellious chickens encountered along the way. And when the Congress assembled, there was a general feeling that the government had done all it could to avoid force; as distasteful as the excise was, it was undeniably constitutional and had to be collected until it could be repealed. The administration's lengthy consideration of the problem before any drastic steps were taken, a consideration imposed by the near-sightedness of the Pennsylvania authorities, fears over whether or not the militia would turn out, and Randolph's arguments in the cabinet, had helped substantially to bring about this general acceptance. If the administration had dashed as precipitately as the "Jersey Blue" had wanted, the public reaction could easily have been quite different. After all the deliberation and delay, or perhaps because of it, the militia's march west became a grand military excursion. At Bedford on October 28, Washington left the force in the command of Governor Henry Lee of Virginia and returned to Philadelphia for the opening of Congress. As the army reached the rebellious area, resistance collapsed and the most prominent leaders fled. Hamilton, representing civil authority, had to content himself with sending twenty obscure "rebels" back to Philadelphia for trial. The evidence against these was so slight that only two were brought to trial; both were convicted, but the President pardoned them for one was insane and the other a simpleton. Despite the tragicomic aspect of its ending, the episode had shown the ability of the government to enforce a duly enacted law and, less obviously, furnished an example of the judicious, prudent application of force.

As Washington rode west with the militia, he became more and more convinced that the troubles were owing to the Democratic Societies;

self-created Societies . . . have been laboring incessantly to sow the seeds of distrust, jealousy, and of course discontent; thereby hoping to effect some revolution in the government. . . . That they have been the fomenters of the Western disturbances, admits of no doubt. . . . I shall be more prolix in my speech to Congress

than usual. In the speech, delivered on November 19, he amply redeemed his promise to be "prolix" on the supposed connection between the Whiskey Rebellion and the Democratic Societies, devoting about 2,000 words out of a total of about 2,500 in the address. The Rebellion was ascribed to "certain self-created societies" and its participants were not simply resisting a tax, but "a spirit inimical to all order has actuated many of the offenders." In concluding his consideration, Washington put it to the citizens generally to

determine, whether it has not been fomented by combinations of men, who, careless of consequences, and disregarding the unerring truth, that those who rouse, can not always appease a civil convulsion, have disseminated, from an ignorance or perversion of facts, suspicions, jealousies, and accusations of the *whole Government* [emph. added].

Thus the president clearly indicated to the public his belief that the Democratic Societies at best served no useful purpose and at worst were bent upon bringing the Constitution and the government conducted under it into such disrepute that it would fall.

Noticeably lacking from the address was any extensive reference to the topics which had so excited the last session of Congress, relations with England and France. Genet's successor, Joseph Fauchet, was still a pleasant contrast to his predecessor, who was now living quietly on Long Island, having married a daughter of Governor Clinton. With England, there was little to report. Randolph had received several vague letters from Jay which made it look as if he was about to conclude a most unsatisfactory treaty; no matter how vain they might be, the secretary immediately wrote correcting instructions and hoped they might arrive in time.

Thus far Washington had had to make only one major replacement in his Cabinet, that of Randolph for Jefferson; the former's post was filled by Andrew Bradford, a Pennsylvania jurist who performed his duties adequately. Now, within one year, Washington had to make three major appointments. After almost ten years, first for the old Congress, then for the new government, Knox wanted to retire and the president could not resist the request. He appointed Timothy Pickering, a dour and opinionated New Englander, then serving as postmaster-general. Pickering had been an officer during the war, compiling the first drill manual used by the Continental forces and serving on Washington's staff during the siege of Yorktown. Hamilton's successor was as close at hand. When the New Yorker left in January 1795, pleading the necessity of looking after his private finances instead of the nation's, he was replaced by the Controller of the Treasury, Oliver Wolcott, Jr. Of a prominent Connecticut family, Wolcott promised competence but not much more in the performance of his duties. These men were Federalists of Hamilton's persuasion and ultimately looked to him rather than to the president as the final arbiter of national questions. Now, of the original 1789 appointees, only Randolph was left and only Randolph tried to be politically independent of both Federalists and Republicans. Despised by the Federalists, who believed him to be yet another of the wild Republicans sent to the capital by Virginia, he was also distrusted by the Republicans, who saw his independent role as either crypto-Federalism or indecisive neutralism. Indeed, a neutral role was becoming increasingly harder to maintain as the parties rapidly crystallized; neither group trusted the uncommitted. Randolph was about to face the greatest crisis of his career without the support a strong political base would have given him; without it he was destroyed and Washington lost the last non-Federalist voice in his Cabinet. The conviction of a French conspiracy using disloyal Americans and putting at peril American freedom was now impressed upon the president.[13]

Randolph's difficulties came, as so many others' did, from London, where Jay had been working to resolve the difficulties in Anglo-American relations. The treaty he negotiated did fulfill the essential point of his instructions, to keep the peace, but it did so only by compromising American interests and the French alliance. It may be true, as some historians have claimed, that Jay got the best possible treaty from the English; it is certainly true that any English treaty would have been scathingly criticized by the Republicans, but Jay's Treaty was so one-sided that even the Federalist-controlled Senate could not accept it as it came to them.

Washington had waited vainly during the congressional session for a copy of the completed treaty; shortly before its adjournment, he called the Senate into special session on June 8 for "certain matters touching the public good," expecting that by then the treaty would have arrived. The suspense and uncertainty ended a few days later, March 7, when a copy finally arrived at the State Department. A quick reading disclosed no concessions by England to the United States but many concessions by the United States to England. By the treaty England was permitted to continue treating American neutral commerce as she had since the war's beginning, but at least in the past the United States had been able to protest these practices against a better day when she might be able to prevent them by her naval strength; this would no longer be possible. Article Eighteen permitted the English to purchase preemptively all provisions declared to be contraband; thus England could keep the French from obtaining American wheat except at her sufferance. Article Twelve did permit American vessels to trade with the British West Indies but under such restrictive conditions that the Senate rejected the article; ships could be no larger than seventy tons—"canoes," as Madison aptly called them—and the United States could not reexport certain tropical commodities; this was designed to end the American reexport trade by which English restrictions were avoided. The English also secured free trade privileges in the Northwest, the use of the Mississippi, and an American promise to pay debts owed by Americans since before the War for Independence. On their part, the English had promised to evacuate the military posts by July 1796; this was hardly much of a concession as that promise had initially been made, and not kept, by the English in the Treaty of 1783. Further, England agreed to submit the ship seizures of the previous winter to arbitration but the United States agreed to do the same for the seizures made by Genet's privateers, so, in principle if not in scope, these canceled each other out. American traders were admitted to the Canadian West but the exclusion of the Hudson's Bay Company territory made this concession meaningless, as that was the most lucrative area. Finally, it could be said that the very fact of England's signing a treaty with the United States was a belated recognition of American nationality and independence from her former colonial overlord, but a patriot would have to be fainthearted indeed to take much cheer from that.

And Washington and Randolph did not take any cheer at all from it. The treaty was accompanied by a self-satisfied letter from Jay proclaiming that his work "must speak for itself. . . . To do more was not possible." The president decided to keep the treaty secret until the Senate convened; by then Jay might be home with an explanation of some of the more exceptionable provisions. The secrecy fed press speculation and Washington might have been amused as one ill-founded rumor after another chased the truth. When Jay arrived in late April, he landed in New York. In his absence he had been elected governor of the state and he resigned his Supreme Court seat by letter, explaining to Randolph that he was much too tired to come to Philadelphia. His answers to a series of questions sent by the secretary were brief and uninformative. Since its negotiator would not, the treaty would have to speak for itself.

Certainly, Washington did not speak for it; the treaty was sent to the Senate with a formal and unrevealing letter of transmission, Jay's original instructions and most of the correspondence between him and Randolph, nothing more. The Senate, during the three weeks it deliberated, kept its debates, and the treaty, secret and, in the end, approved it by the barest margin possible, twenty to ten. But in so doing, Washington was given two dilemmas: now that the treaty was consented to, should he go ahead and ratify it? And since the Senate had omitted Article Twelve, should a new one be negotiated and resubmitted or should it be inserted with no further action by the Senate? While the president pondered this, he directed Randolph to release the treaty to the press. Unfortunately, while copies were being prepared, Senator Stevens Mason of Virginia took it upon himself to give a copy to Benjamin Franklin Bache, the fiercely Republican editor of the *Aurora* who immediately published it in pamphlet form. Thus the administration looked as if it had tried to keep the treaty a secret until the president had ratified it.

The Cabinet advised Washington to sign the treaty but he delayed a bit, waiting for an opinion from Hamilton which he had requested. As he waited, he learned that the English had begun to confiscate—not purchase preemptively but confiscate—provision cargoes destined for France. Was England intent on securing free what she would have to pay for after ratification? Or was this an indication that the promises made in Jay's treaty were no more reliable than some made in the 1783 treaty? Randolph suggested and Washington agreed that the secretary inform the English minister that the president would ratify the treaty, Article Twelve excepted, just as soon as the order confiscating provisions was withdrawn, but no sooner. On July 13, he told Randolph he was irrevocably committed to this procedure.[14]

Two days later Washington took Martha south to Mount Vernon to escape the "suffocating" climate of Philadelphia. Into that calm atmosphere, the fast-breaking controversy over the treaty began to penetrate. The president complained that party disputes were so muddying the waters that one could determine the truth only with difficulty; inferentially, Republican criticism of the treaty was the problem. He blamed its critics for the "most tortured interpretations and . . . the most abominable misrepresentations" of it and confided to Hamilton that some of their activity was certainly owing to French influence. He also commented favorably on the protreaty "Camillus" essays which had started to appear; he may have realized he was writing to their author, for he contrasted the author's activity with the usual inactivity of the "friends of order and good government." The intense and bitter controversy over the treaty was affecting Washington, and his latent sympathy for Federalism was starting to surface.

As he was preparing to return to Philadelphia, he received a request from Randolph that he come back as soon as possible; the Cabinet had unanimously decided that he was needed there. But accompanying this was a mysterious note from Pickering marked "for your eye alone" and confiding that "on the subject of the treaty I confess that I feel extreme solicitude, and for *a special reason* [orig. emph.]" which could be given to the president only in person. He must often have wondered what could have gotten the Yankee into such a fret until he reached the capital on August 11. Pickering came that afternoon and found Washington and Randolph at table; excusing himself the president took Pickering into another room. As soon as the door closed, the Secretary of War melodramatically pointed toward the dining room and flatly stated: "That man is a traitor!"[15]

He explained briefly that the English had turned over a captured French diplomatic dispatch to Wolcott, who had given it to him; according to Pickering's translation, the dispatch stated that Randolph had approached Fauchet with an offer to influence American foreign policy in return for money. Randolph's well-known financial difficulties made the charge credible and Washington was probably able only to nod dumbly as he was told that Wolcott would bring the relevant documents that evening. Later, after he had read them over, he saw that Fauchet's statements could support Pickering's charge. His closest associate and the only member of the 1789 Cabinet to stay the distance had possibly betrayed his country.[16]

The effect of this on Washington can hardly be underestimated. He had known Randolph since the war; during the 1780s the young man had performed many legal tasks for the retired general, never charging a fee. Lacking a son of his own, the older man frequently solicitously dominated the younger men around him; there is nothing to show that Randolph resented this. Indeed, in July, he had told the president that he could not foresee staying on in any successor's administration; his only purpose was to serve Washington, and he could not work so closely with anyone else. In turn, the president had recognized the valuable services his Secretary of State was performing and was increasingly relying on him as his principal advisor. Now he discovered that there was apparently good reason to distrust that advice; if he could not trust Randolph, whom could he trust?

On August 12 Washington called the Cabinet together and suggested that the treaty be ratified immediately and unconditionally. Randolph had a memorial defending a delayed and conditional ratification ready and, despite his surprise at Washington's unexplained about-face, defended it against a united opposition. When he had finished, the president, with no further comment, declared: "I will ratify the treaty," and ordered Randolph to prepare the necessary papers. Thus the English had succeeded in one of their major purposes in turning the dispatch over, to remove Washington's respect for Randolph whom they had tabbed as the only anti-English member of the Cabinet. It now remained to complete their plan by removing him from the Cabinet entirely. For the next week the president and the Secretary of State met frequently, going over the anticonfiscation memorial and the draft ratification certificates. In none of these meetings did Washington give Randolph any hint that he distrusted him and, if he gave any explanation for his sudden reversal, it was probably that only an immediate ratification would end the harsh public controversy which now focused upon Washington. By August 18 all the necessary documents had been prepared and the president ratified the treaty. Under the circumstances, it is clear that he signed it when he did only because of the allegations which had been made against Randolph on the basis of the captured dispatch. The Secretary of State had been the only one in the Cabinet arguing against immediate ratification; if Washington's independence of judgment had not disappeared, it had certainly been seriously compromised.

The next day, in the presence of Wolcott and Pickering, Washington confronted Randolph with the captured dispatch: "Mr. Randolph, here is a letter which I desire you to read, and make such explanations as you choose." After he had finished, Randolph offered to make as good an explanation as he could from memory only. After he had made what Wolcott called a "desultory" answer, an apparently unflustered Randolph was asked to leave the room while the other three talked it over. But when he came back, his calmness was gone and he answered sharply some perfunctory questions before interrupting with a statement that he could no lónger remain in office. He left immediately, went to the State Department, where he locked his room, leaving the key with the clerk, and went home, where he wrote his formal letter of resignation. In it he denied ever asking for or receiving any money from Fauchet and gave what seems to be the most likely explanation for his resignation:

Your confidence, in me, Sir, has been unlimited and, I can truly affirm, unabused. My sensations, then, cannot be concealed when I find that confidence so immediately withdrawn without a word or distant hint being previously dropped to me! This, Sir, as I mentioned in your room, is a situation in which I cannot hold my present office, and therefore I hereby resign it.

In his acknowledgment, Washington expressed no regret for what had happened, simply explaining to Randolph how the document had come to him and agreeing to the latter's request that the affair be kept confidential until he could prepare a vindication. Now Washington was left with an exclusively Federalist corps of advisors. Once he had confided to Lear his concern that he was too "stationary" and did not hear enough different opinions; now even Lear was gone (he had resigned in 1793 to go into business) and Washington no longer seemed concerned that he was "stationary."[17]

Randolph's *Vindication* appeared in December; a solid presentation of the evidence, it nevertheless failed to change his enemies' minds or even reassure his friends as to his innocence. His major mistake was to concentrate on proving himself the victim of an English plot—he was, but neither he nor anyone else in America had the evidence to prove that—instead of explaining exactly what Fauchet had meant by the incriminating phrases in the captured dispatch. Presently Randolph fell into obscurity, an obscurity from which he emerged from time to time as an embarrassing reminder to the Federalists and Republicans of the casualties of their party warfare.[18]

Washington asked Pickering to take over the State Department while he searched for a permanent successor to Randolph. Then, somewhat in the fashion of the bridegroom's father in the New Testament parable, he heard excuses, some real, some invented, from five men as to why they could not take the position. Finally, probably in desperation, he offered it to Pickering, who had to be talked into accepting it by Wolcott. This left only the War Department, as Charles Lee of Virginia had just agreed to replace Bradford, who had died, as attorney-general. A letter from James McHenry recommending a fellow Marylander, Samuel Chase, for a Supreme Court vacancy, elicited not only Washington's acceptance of Chase but also an offer of the War Department to McHenry. His acceptance along with Oliver Ellsworth's of the Chief Justiceship meant that Washington began the last full year of his presidency with no major offices unfilled, but John Adams's comment on this was very much to the point: "The offices are once more filled, but how differently than when Jefferson, Hamilton, Jay, etc., were here."[19] How differently indeed. None of the new appointees was a first-rate man; all were firm Federalists.

Shortly after Randolph left office, Washington clearly signaled that he had no regrets about the treaty, whatever emotions he might have left unvoiced about his ex-secretary. Answering a memorial against the treaty from some Savannah citizens in mid-September he assured them that in considering the treaty he was guided "by the great principle which has governed all my public conduct: a sincere desire to promote and secure the true interests of my country." In other words, he would do his duty as he saw it, regardless of public opinion. A few weeks later, he told Knox that as he had found no better "guide than upright intentions and close investigation, I shall adhere to these maxims while I keep the watch." The point might well be made as to how clearly he was seeing the interests of the country and how much close investigation public matters were receiving. But the watch was certainly drawing to a close.

Washington returned to Philadelphia on October 20 from a visit to Mount Vernon; in the capital he felt the full blast of the uproar over his signing of the treaty, without any of the filtering effect which the calmness and serenity of his Virginia home gave. For example, on the twenty-first, "Valerius" in the *Aurora* gave him no credit for any act of his public life and concluded that the American people well knew that "nature had played the miser when she gave you birth" and "education had not been lavish in her favours." Slurs of this sort could be, but probably were not, laughed off. After the treaty had been approved, Republican criticism of the administration was directed much more toward Washington than it had ever been before; it was now designed to make certain that Washington did not stand for election in 1796, a decision which his critics never imagined he had made in 1792. Republican criticism hit very close to home on the twenty-third when "A Calm Observer" alleged that Washington had overdrawn his salary account; unfortunately for his composure and his concern about his reputation, the charges were true. There were several mitigating factors, carefully explained by Wolcott and his predecessor, not the least of which was that the president had never been aware of the advances. Republican editors brushed aside the explanations and delightedly repeated their basic point: Washington had overdrawn his salary. Yet this was a kind of postscript to the treaty controversy; it had been going on since spring and was visibly winding down. [20]

Washington may have realized this when he gave his annual message to the Congress on December. 8. He began on a high note of congratulation and celebration and, with rare exceptions, maintained it. A peace with the Northern Indians had recently been concluded and negotiations with the Southern tribes were going well; a satisfactory treaty with the Barbary states was expected soon and Thomas Pinckney, treating with the Spanish in Madrid, had reported substantial progress. Jay's Treaty was only glanced at by the assurance that when English ratification was known, Congress would be immediately notified. Then, speaking generally of foreign and Indian affairs Washington said:

If by prudence and moderation on every side, the extinguishment of all the causes of external discord, which have heretofore menaced our tranquility, on terms compatible with our national rights and honor, shall be the happy result; how firm and how precious a foundation will have been laid for accelerating, maturing, and establishing the prosperity of our country!

The balance of the address dealt with domestic affairs, and in much the same tone. This was simply reiterating a theme he had used frequently when he was trying to keep the peace between Jefferson and Hamilton: if Americans would only compose their differences, the future alone guaranteed the greatness and strength of their republic. In the partisan atmosphere of 1795 this impressed relatively few Americans of either party, but for a time there was political peace.

In this mood, Washington accepted from the new French minister, Pierre Adet, a richly ornamented tricolor flag, a return for an American flag given to the French Assembly by Monroe and hung in their chamber. The president thanked Adet and noted that "to call your nation brave, were to pronounce but common praise. Wonderful people! Ages to come will read with astonishment the history of your brilliant exploits," and informed the minister that the banner would be put in the "archives" of the United States. In other words, a dusty corner of the State Department, not the hall of the House of Representatives. Adet noticed and resented this, but Congress did not.

The mood was maintained a while longer by receipt of a draft treaty from Thomas Pinckney. During Jay's stay in London, he had been relieved of his duties there and sent to Spain to seek a settlement of several outstanding matters. Partly because of European conditions, partly because of fear that Jay's Treaty might hide an Anglo-American alliance, the Spanish gave the Americans a very generous settlement which the Senate unanimously approved on March 3.[21] This marked the end of the cheer and good fellowship. Washington had been waiting impatiently for receipt of the certificates of ratification from London but they had been delayed by the inexperience of the American chargé there. On the strength of private reports that the treaty had been ratified in London, Washington declared it in effect on February 29. Since the treaty provided for several arbitration commissions whose expenses were shared by the signatories, Congress now had to appropriate money to carry it into effect. Appropriation bills customarily originated in the House and that is where the fun started on March 2.

Washington predicted that, now that the Republicans had a second chance at the treaty, "an attempt . . . will be made to censure it in several points"—more than several points. Edward Livingston of New York immediately asked the House to request delivery of all papers relevant to the negotiations, since "important constitutional questions" were raised by the treaty. The implications here were obvious and significant; only the president and the Senate made treaties; the House had no role. While in the past Washington had implicitly recognized that the House's assent was sometimes necessary in practice, this was far different from permitting it to set aside a properly ratified treaty. The House debated the motion for almost three weeks before passing it, softened somewhat, sixty-two to thirty-seven. Anticipating the action, Washington had already asked for advice. He had honored some calls for papers previously but treaties had never been involved. The Cabinet and Hamilton advised him not to comply with the call and he readily agreed. Basing his refusal on expediency and the Constitution, he wrote:

The nature of foreign negotiations requires caution and their success must often depend on secrecy . . . a full disclosure of all the measures, demands or eventual concessions . . . would be extremely impolitic. . . . It does not occur that the inspection of the papers . . . can be relative to any purpose under the [Constitutional] cognizance of the House. . . . It is perfectly clear to my understanding that the assent of the House . . . is not necessary to the validity of a treaty. . . .

Many Republicans had expected a partial compliance by the president in keeping with the now-vanished mood of political reconciliation and were shocked by his complete refusal. No one expected the Republicans to fold their tents and ride away, but Washington now challenged them by sending nominations for the arbitration commissions to the Senate for confirmation. Against the president's firm determination to execute the treaty, the House had a weapon of unsurpassing effectiveness, inaction. If it did not vote the appropriations, the commissioners would not be paid and at least part of the treaty would be voided. Both the House and the public debated the question for all of April; contrary to the previous summer, this time there seemed to be a slim popular majority in favor of execution. Public opinion, the difficulties which would come from repudiating the treaty, the likelihood that England would refuse to hand over the posts, scheduled to be surrendered in June, talk of a war with England just when France was said to be mistreating American commerce—all combined to break down the Republican majority and the House voted, on April 29, to accept the president's reply to Livingston's resolution. In several more close votes, the appropriations were passed.

In retrospect, Washington decided that the Republicans were not questioning the value of Jay's Treaty as much as they were trying to increase the power of the House with its Republican majority. Why they had tried to do this also interested him. "Charity would lead one to hope that the motives to it have been pure. Suspicions, however, speak a different language; and my tongue, for present, shall be silent." The people could decide correctly if only certain leaders, "adverse to the Government," would stop bending all their efforts to mislead them. "To this source all our discontents may be traced, and from it our embarrassments proceed." No credit was given to the treaty's opponents for acting, however mistakenly, in good faith. Washington was one with Hamilton and other leaders of Federalism in suspecting the Republicans of playing the French game. The president went so far as to credit a fantastic rumor sent home by Gouverneur Morris that the French were sending a new envoy accompanied by a battle fleet and a demand that Jay's Treaty be repudiated within fifteen days, although he did wonder that "folly and madness would hardly go such lengths."

Whatever his thoughts on the perfidy of the French, he could easily distract himself with a more pleasant prospect, his retirement in less than a year. Even before the question of the Jay's Treaty appropriations had been decided, he had discussed with Hamilton, who had become his principal political advisor, how best his decision not to accept reelection might be announced. Hamilton had offered his editorial assistance in preparing a letter to the people and most of the summer was spent passing back and forth between Philadelphia and New York drafts and revisions. The first draft, prepared entirely by Washington, was a revealing document which showed how much the party animosities and newspaper attacks had injured his feelings and his need to be seen as the universally accepted leader of the people. For example, he mentioned his refusal to accept a salary during the war and his unwillingness to take it during the presidency and that his service had actually cost him money. He further commented that he had never sought office nor had he accepted it out of personal ambition or ignorance of its responsibilities. After a paragraph complaining of newspaper attacks, he wrote: "It might be expected at the parting scene of my public life that I should take some notice of such virulent abuse. But, as heretofore, I shall pass them over in utter silence," having written several dozen words about them. His own good sense must have told him that this would not do, as he asked Hamilton to prune it of any "egotisms" it might contain. In the joint work of composition and revision, the message was changed and lengthened considerably, but it remained Washington's. Where Hamilton tried to slip something in which the President did not approve, it was noticed and thrown out; for instance, where

Hamilton prophesied that if the government fell, it would be because of its excessive weakness, Washington crossed the lines out. The finished product does help to show how much of a Federalist Washington had become during his second term; although Hamilton wrote most of the Farewell Address, Washington accepted it and put it out as his own.[22]

Generations of Americans have been accustomed to reading or thinking—few have actually read it—of the Farewell Address as the first chapter of a kind of catechism of American politics and foreign policy. Read outside the times in which it was written, that is understandable. But if one recalls the circumstances of the summer of 1796, the address becomes a Federalist campaign speech, putting the stamp of Washington's approval upon Federalist ideas and policies. The address begins with sentiments suitable for a leave-taking but then, where it could end, the president comments: "Here, perhaps, I ought to stop." But his concern for the welfare of the country leads him to offer "some sentiments . . . which appear to me all-important to the permanency of your felicity as a People." He then proceeds to dwell on the importance of the Union, religion and morality as props of society, the value of true neutrality, and the necessity of a proper regard for the public credit. Many of these are unexceptionable and some of timeless importance. But the best-remembered injunctions were the ones which were the most partisan in their implications. When Washington cautioned Americans to avoid "permanent alliances," he was talking to a nation which had had only one such alliance in its short life, with France, a nation which was showing scant regard for the interests of its supposed ally. When he urged his fellow citizens to avoid extreme and fixed feelings about a foreign country, he was talking to a people who had heard frequent warnings during the Jay's Treaty controversy from the Federalists that Republican opposition to the treaty was a product of their unreasoning antipathy to England and their uncritical attachment to France. When he warned that political parties brought foreign influences to bear on domestic questions, he was warning a people who had recently seen the French minister send his government's messages to the Secretary of State the same day they were published in the *Aurora*, in translation, and who well remembered Citizen Genet. Thus the address can be seen as the opening gun of a campaign to elect a Federalist president in 1796. That the gun was fired by a man who sincerely felt himself above parties adds to the irony of the situation; men do not always see themselves clearly.[23]

Washington had originally hoped to see the valedictory in print shortly after Congress adjourned in the spring but other matters intruded and presently early fall, at least two months before the electors met, was set as the target. On September 16, the President called in David Claypoole of the *American Daily Advertiser* and asked him to "usher it to the world and suffer it to work its way afterwards." The address was published on the nineteenth, the same day Washington left for Mount Vernon, where Bartholomew Dandridge wrote his uncle "that not a single instance of disapprobation of any part thereof has been found. . . . All seem to agree in the solid truths which the address contains." Either Dandridge was sparing his uncle's feelings or he did not look very hard. The *Boston Gazette* rejoiced that now Americans could look forward to a time when political "Principles will be investigated *unclouded by Names* [orig. emph.]," in other words, free of Washington's influence. Actually, reaction divided pretty much along party lines, although most Republicans paid at least lip service to Washington's contributions. [24]

The president returned to Philadelphia at the end of October to find a complaint from the French on his desk (and in the pages of the *Aurora*). They complained that their observance of the 1778 treaties placed them at a disadvantage to the English because of the latter's special privileges under Jay's Treaty. There was some justice to the complaint but Washington and Pickering would hear none of it. In his reply, Pickering informed the French that there were two kinds of international law, the standard variety and that which resulted from treaties. Only the former bound the United States and England while the latter bound France and the United States. Simply because France's obligations were inconvenient did not mean that they could be set aside. [25] Washington himself observed that there was "in the conduct of the French government . . . an inconsistency, a duplicity, a delay or something else which is unaccountable upon honorable ground." This from a man who had observed in 1791 that nations would obey treaties only as long as it was in their interest to do so.

Washington probably was not blaming the French entirely for the trouble. James Monroe had become, in the eyes of the administration, more and more partisan in the conduct of his ministry in Paris. Recently Pickering had intercepted (how is not clear) a letter from Monroe to a Philadelphia friend giving the "real" news from Paris, not the distorted version copied out of English newspapers by the Federalist press. It was obviously destined for the pages of the *Aurora*, and there was the promise of more to follow. The conviction had already been growing that Monroe was representing the Republican party, not the United States, in Paris and that he had given the French the mistaken impression that American foreign policy was the creation of a small and unrepresentative clique. His recall was decided upon and Thomas Pinckney's brother, Charles Cotesworth, was asked to take up the post. Monroe had really been doing a good job of representing the United States to a government which felt itself severely injured by Jay's Treaty; Pinckney would now set the French straight.[26]

As the Farewell Address was being allowed to "work its way," Washington turned to the preparation of his eighth and last Annual Message to Congress. The farewell had, deliberately been kept general because of its audience; as he was now, in effect, saying good-bye to Congress, he took the occasion to remind them of a number of items previously presented which he still thought important along with several new topics for legislation. When he came to foreign relations, however, his treatment strongly contrasted with previous messages; where he had always tried to be even-handed before, he now permitted an obvious displeasure with the French treatment of American commerce in the West Indies to show although little was said for fear of a charge of trying to influence the election. A special message, to be given at a later time, would treat the topic in detail. Relations with England received a very different treatment; even that power's lateness in handing over the military posts was depicted as necessary and excusable. But the treatment of domestic items showed some of Washington's anxieties about the durability of the peace; he urged immediate planning for the construction of a strong navy and for government aid or direct manufacture of items necessary for defense which could not be supplied domestically. He also urged government sponsorship of boards charged with the support and improvement of agriculture, an object of "primary importance" to the nation's welfare, and the payment of higher salaries to government officials; "it would be repugnant to the vital principles of our Government, virtually to exclude from public trusts, talents and virtue, unless accompanied by wealth."

A much larger than usual audience attended when Washington delivered the Message on December 7, as it was the last time when most could reasonably expect to see the man already generally referred to as the Father of his Country. Henrietta Liston, the perceptive wife of the English minister, noticed "the extreme agitation He felt when He mentioned the *French* [orig. emph.]. He is, I believe, very much inraged." Mrs. Liston would presently write of the only vain remark she ever heared Washington make, that his face never betrayed his emotions—vain and incorrect.[27] She also noted the audience's emotion as the president concluded his talk:

The situation in which I now stand, for the last time, in the midst of the Representatives of the People of the United States, naturally recalls the period when the Administration of the present form of Government commenced; and I cannot omit the occasion, to congratulate you and my Country, on the success of the experiment; nor to repeat my fervent supplications to the Supreme Ruler of the Universe, and Sovereign Arbiter of Nations, that his Providential care may still be extended to the United States; that the virtue and happiness of the People may be preserved; and that the Government, which they have instituted for the protection of their liberties, may be perpetual.

His last major public appearance as president behind him, Washington was free to concentrate on the election; although he wrote nothing to betray his interest, it can be assumed that he was gratified to see Adams squeak out a three-vote victory in the Electoral College over Jefferson, who thus became vice-president. Recently Washington had seen a good bit more of his vice-president than earlier, when he had suffered a kind of semiexile because of his presumed championing of the form, and substance, of monarchy. Adams was pleased to note the similarity of views between himself and the president, a similarity of which the latter must also have been aware. But Washington probably did not see Adams's independence, an independence which would not permit him to ask more of the French than of the English and which gave him a tumultuous and, ultimately, frustrating administration.

Washington was not ready to be so evenhanded. In preparing the special message on relations with France, the Secretary of State was instructed to point to the United States' "fair dealing towards all the Belligerent Powers," and to say further that, "wrapt up in its own integrity," it had not anticipated the ill treatment it had received from France. The administration was certain, Washington went on, that France would realize this also and offer compensation for vessels recently seized in the West Indies. But, whether France realized it or not, there would be no change of U.S. policy. The message took the form of instructions to Minister Pinckney who, in his dealings with the French, who considered themselves to be the injured party, was charged to ask for more and offer nothing, not even consoling phrases.

As the last days of his administration wound themselves out, Washington's name became more and more an object of scorn in the Republican press, which published an open letter from Tom Paine, who felt, for various reasons, that the president had wronged him. Speaking out of his hurt and his disappointment at affairs in both of his adopted countries, America and France, Paine questioned whether Washington had ever had "good principles" or had recently abandoned even the pretense of them. Bache joined eagerly in the chorus and, on the day of Adams's inauguration, rejoiced that

the man who is the source of all the misfortunes of our country is this day reduced to a level with his fellow citizens, and is no longer possesst of power to multiply evils upon the United States. . . . The name of Washington ceases from this day to give currency to political iniquity and to legalize corruption.

Within Bache's hyperbole, there nevertheless was a grudging and implicit acceptance of a point made earlier by Mrs. Liston when she learned of Washington's decision to retire: "There is a Magic in his name more powerful than the Abilities of any other man can ever acquire." The violence of Bache's language testified more convincingly to this "Magic" than any of the hymns of praise being turned out by Federalists could.[28]

The inauguration of the second President of the United States took place on Saturday, March 4, 1797, in Congress Hall. The first president, dressed in a simple black suit, walked alone to the hall while a splendidly dressed Adams rode over in a new carriage. At the conclusion of the brief ceremony, Washington stepped forward and congratulated Adams, who probably came closer than anyone else to capturing his predecessor's feelings when he wrote: "He seemed to enjoy a triumph over me. Methought I heard him say, 'Ay! I am fairly out and you fairly in! See which of us will be happiest!'"[29] Washington emphasized his new status by refusing to walk out ahead of the new vice-president but instead standing aside until the tall Virginian reluctantly went ahead of his former chief; then George Washington, private citizen, left the hall.

CHAPTER 7

The Final Commission, 1797–1799

I see, as you do, that clouds are gathering and that a storm may ensue. . . . [It
will be both painful and necessary] to quit the tranquil walks of retirement
and enter the boundless field of responsibility and trouble.

WITH Adams's inauguration, Washington might have ceased
being a public servant, but he was still very much a public
person and that night a farewell banquet was held in a hall decorated
by a transparency depicting Washington being crowned by "Fame."
A round of farewell visits and the necessary packing then took almost
a week before the family was ready to leave. Last-minute chores were
assumed by Lear, who had returned to the general's employ. Even
with his help, items were forgotten or misplaced, not all to Washington's displeasure, for as he confided to Lear: "On one side I am called
upon to remember the Parrot, on the other to remember the dog. For
my own part I should not pine much if both were forgot."[1] No matter
how different the conditions or eminent the persons, moving a family
(Martha's grandchildren owned the pets) always seems to have been a
bothersome chore. Dog, parrot, furniture, and people eventually all
arrived safely on the Potomac, with the people getting there first, on
March 14.

As in 1783, Washington settled back quickly into the routine of the
plantation; and again, as in 1783, he discovered much to be done.
Despite his visits and the services of a series of managers—James
Anderson, a Scot, was the incumbent—the lands and the buildings
showed the absence of their owner's care. Soon the mansion house
began to resound with the bang of hammers while the odor of paint
overbore all the pleasant smells of a burgeoning Virginia spring. The
only new construction ordered was a small outbuilding to house his
official papers which, their owner explained with characteristic
understatement, "are voluminous, and may be interesting." He
described his routine to McHenry, who had promised to keep him
informed on national affairs:

I begin my diurnal course with the sun; that if my hirelings are not in their places at that time I send them messages expressive of my sorrow for their indisposition; then having put these wheels in motion, I examine the state of things further; and the more they are probed, the deeper I find the wounds are which my buildings have sustained by an absence and neglect of eight years; by the time I have accomplished these matters, breakfast—a little after seven o'clock . . . is ready. This over, I mount my horse and ride around the farms, which employs me until it is time to dress for dinner. . . The usual time of sitting at Table, a walk, and Tea, brings me within the dawn of Candlelight; previous to which, if not prevented by company, I resolve that, as soon as the glimmering taper, supplies the place of the great luminary, I will retire to my writing Table and acknowledge the letters I have received; but when the lights are brought, I feel tired, and disinclined to engage in this work, conceiving that the next night will do as well: the next comes and with it the same causes for postponement . . . and so on.

This passage, expressive of the deep contentment Washington always found at Mount Vernon, did not tell the whole story.

His finances were in almost as much disarray as his buildings. During the presidential years, he had spent his salary and more maintaining the house in Philadelphia, with the income from Mount Vernon just sufficient to pay its expenses. Confronting the expenses of the Mount Vernon repairs and the increased cost of entertaining the steady stream of visitors come to pay their respects (the old gentlemen wondered: "Pray, would not the word curiosity answer as well?"), Washington accepted the offer of a glib-talking land speculator, James Welch, for a long-term lease of some 23,000 acres of his Kanawha lands. The rent, computed as 6 percent interest on $200,000, would be a welcome supplement to the income which the improved management of Mount Vernon might yield. Unfortunately Welch's words were more impressive than his accomplishment and the rent never materialized. Other transactions were more successful and, in 1799, he estimated that he had realized approximately $50,000 during the last five years; except for this income, he would have been in serious debt; as it was, even with the land sales, Washington never solved what modern accountants would call a "cash-flow" problem. For this he was partially responsible, for he could never bring himself to sue his creditors for repayment or even press them hard. His letters requesting payment almost always contained an extensive description of his own sad financial condition, and they often sounded like those he had written to the old Congress during the war. Nor did he find it easy to cut down his expenditures.

Indeed, he even increased them and in 1798 began the construction of two houses near the site of the Capitol in Washington. To complete the project, he was driven, for the first time in his life, to borrow $2,500 from an Alexandria bank at what he thought was "a ruinous interest." Despite his shortage of ready cash, Washington was a successful land speculator. Anyone who could realize $50,000 and still have thousands of acres left had not done badly at all. At his death, he valued his real-estate holdings at almost half a million dollars. The major reason for his success was that he had been able to avoid going into debt to acquire his lands; with low or nonexistent taxes, he was easily able to hold on to them while they appreciated.

His money troubles may have been partially responsible for his plans to lease his farms and free his slaves, plans which also grew out of an increasing repugnance to the institution. Fortunately he had kept this feeling to himself, fortunate as it would have antagonized most of the South and prevented him from leading the nation as its first president. But he could not stop thinking about how to deal with the problem. He proposed to lease the farms to English farmers (American farmers were too wasteful and tied up with slavery) and use the income to support himself and those slaves who were unable to care for themselves; the rest would be freed. The two parts of the plan depended upon each other, and the project fell through when no prospective lessors presented themselves. Except for some house servants who were allowed to stay behind in Philadelphia, Washington kept his slaves until he died. His will provided that all of them would be freed at Martha's death, as their labor was needed to work the farms and support her. This proved impracticable, as the slaves soon learned of the proviso and her children feared what might happen with 300 blacks waiting for the old woman to die. They were freed in 1801 except for those who were too old to work. The episode is typical of Washington's manner of dealing with problems; he only moved to alleviate them if a feasible solution presented itself. If you could not solve the difficulty, you lived with it.[2]

Problems or no, Washington still found retirement to be as gratifying as he had expected. Mrs. Liston had commented earlier that he should not be acclaimed for stepping down, as he was only satisfying his deepest desire. Thus, when she and her husband visited Mount Vernon in December 1797, they found the old man "improved by retirement like a Man relieved from a heavy burthen. He has thrown off a little that prudence which formerly guarded his every word . . . he converses with the more ease and cheerfulness."[3]

Others noted the same change; now that he no longer spoke for the nation, he was freer in speaking for himself. When his wartime aide, the Marquis de Lafayette, had been put in prison because of the shifting tides of the French Revolution, the president had done all he could privately, for example, sending a sum of money to Madame de Lafayette, but doing nothing publicly which might offend the French. Near the end of his term, however, he brought the marquis's son, George Washington Lafayette, and his tutor, who had come to the United States some time before, to live in his family, his first public kindness to the young man. The youngster left Mount Vernon in October 1797 as soon as he had learned of his father's release from prison, carrying an invitation to visit the plantation where Washington could receive the marquis as his private feelings and not his public position dictated.

Adding to the pleasure of retirement was the generally good health which Washington enjoyed. Other than getting enough exercise, chiefly by horseback-riding, this was not something he worked very hard at. In October 1798 he answered Landon Carter, who had sent some personal prescriptions for keeping well, by saying, in effect, no thanks. "Having, through life, been blessed with a competent share of [good health], without using preventatives against sickness, and as little medicine as possible when sick; I can have no inducement now to change my practice. against the effect of time and age, no remedy has ever yet been discovered." He hoped he would submit gracefully to the inevitable effects of old age. The same could not be said for Martha, and the general hired a housekeeper to ease the burden of heavy entertaining which seemed to be the Washingtons' lot in life, in or out of office. By this and other kindnesses, Washington showed his high regard for the woman who, although she had not given him any children (and whose fault was that?) had given him comfort and encouragement during the difficult years of the war and had done the same during the presidency without ever embarrassing him by the betrayal of a husbandly confidence or even simply an imprudent statement of a personal opinion which could be taken as reflecting his feelings. None of this was the material for high romance or a novel of romantic love, and Washington confessed as much to Eliza Powel, a close friend of the couple from Philadelphia. She had purchased a desk from them and found in it a packet of letters from Martha to him. Although she returned it unopened, she could not resist teasing him by suggesting what the letters might contain. He assured her that, if she had read them, they would be "more fraught with expressions of friendship, than of *enamoured* [orig. emph.] love."[4] They would have to be burnt to give any warmth. Great romance, no, but a quiet, kindly love, yes.

The reader of several newspapers and, despite his disclaimer to McHenry, an active correspondent with friends throughout the country, Washington knew sooner than most of the French decision not to receive Charles Cotesworth Pinckney. This moved him to confess that French policy was "so much beyond calculation, and so unaccountable upon any principle of justice or even . . . of plain understanding" that he would not even try to understand it. He approved of President Adams's urging of unity against the French at a special session of Congress in May 1797, commenting that "the idea that the Government and the People have different views [should not] be suffered any longer to prevail, at home or abroad." The French needed to see "an unequivocal expression of the public mind," an expression, Washington was certain, which would support his policies, policies which he saw President Adams continuing. He approved sending John Marshall, a Virginia Federalist, and Elbridge Gerry, then passing from Federalism to Republicanism, to Paris to help Pinckney convince the French of their errors. But the new envoys would carry instructions little changed from Pinckney's; the United States still asked much and offered little. Washington saw the problem as stemming from a French misconception of American politics; they still believed they could make the United States do their will by swaying the interests and allegiance of the Republicans. But they were mistaken; "the *Mass* of our Citizens require no more than to understand a question to decide it properly, and an adverse conclusion of the Negotiation will effect this." Taking away the value judgment implicit in "properly," the general's description fit what was to happen rather closely.

Washington showed how strongly he felt about Republican Francophilia when he reacted angrily to Monroe's defense of his conduct in Paris; the defense was contained in a larger work, *A View of the Conduct of the Executive . . . 1794, 5 & 6*, in foreign affairs. Some of the former minister's criticisms were valid, but mostly they worked out to a disapproval of Jay's Treaty. Uncharacteristically, Washington wrote comments in the margin of his copy, holding an angry debate with the author. When Monroe alleged that if the United States had not abandoned France, the latter would have denied America nothing, Washington retorted: "That is to say, if we w[oul]d not press *them* to do us Justice, but had yielded to *their* violations, they would have aided us in every measure which would have cost them: *Nothing* [orig. emph.]." Most of Monroe's other contentions were met with the same untypical spirit of angry sarcasm as Washington filled margin after margin with angry rejoinders. He took every care to note Monroe's mistakes but gave him no credit at all for his accomplishments.[5] Increasingly, in Washington's view, criticism of the administration's actions and policies was an unallowable criticism of the government. With the prospect of increasingly tense relations with France, such an attitude did not indicate that Washington would take kindly to attempts to explain or justify French policy. His mind was made up.

Nor did his comments regarding the ultimate correctness of the people reflect optimism about the immediate future; there were too many obstacles to a "proper" understanding. The Republicans were using "cowardly, illiberal and assasin [*sic*] like" weapons to "subvert" the government's policy and "to destroy all confidence in those who are entrusted with the Administration" of that policy. He was afraid that "misrepresentation and party feuds" might well end in "confusion and anarchy." What had seemed about to occur ten years before, contentions ending in disunion, again seemed to be in prospect. As he celebrated his sixty-sixth birthday, all he could see was "internal dissensions and political hostilities in the councils" of the Republic. Although retired, "I cannot but view these things with deep concern." Much, if not all, depended on what was happening in Paris, but no one on this side of the Atlantic had heard anything about the progress of the mission. By early March, Washington felt that only the guillotine could explain the silence of American delegates in Paris.

But the reason for their silence was much more prosaic. To avoid capture by the English, their dispatches had been sent by a roundabout route which caused them to be bunched up; just as Washington was worrying about the commissioners, their reports were being read in Philadelphia. The story they contained was anything but prosaic. On their arrival in Paris the previous October, the emissaries had been greeted with delaying tactics by the custodian of French foreign policy, Charles Maurice de Talleyrand-Perigord, the renegade Bishop of Autun, who had already adapted himself from the Old Regime to the New and would continue adapting himself until he was serving the restored Bourbon monarchy at the end of the Napoleonic Era. Unofficially, persons claiming to be agents for individuals within the French government approached the Americans and demanded a combination of bribes and a forced loan to the French government before their credentials would be received and negotiations begin. The Americans recognized the possible necessity of paying bribes in the shifting, corrupt atmosphere which pervaded the French capital, but they would pay only for results, not opportunities. This stalemate continued through the spring of 1798 until Marshall and Pinckney were convinced they could accomplish nothing and left Paris; Gerry was assured by Talleyrand that war would follow the end of the mission and stayed until July when he also gave up. The dispatches President Adams received in March told enough of the story to convince him the mission was a failure; this, combined with news of increased French seizures in the West Indies, led Adams to realize he was sitting on a volcano. He tried to buy time by reporting to Congress only that dispatches had been received and revealed no hope "that their mission can be accomplished on terms compatible with the safety, the honor, or the essential interests of the nation." But he recommended only defensive measures, probably expecting the French presently to furnish grounds for war.[6]

Republicans, believing that Adams's vague language concealed a moderate response by the French, combined with extreme Federalists who wanted what they were confident was a sordid tale revealed for all to see, to pass a congressional resolution calling for the dispatches. For once, the Federalists' hopes were gratified and the Republicans could not resist a joint resolution for publication. In releasing the dispatches to Congress, President Adams had replaced the French agents' names with initial letters and so, by mid-April, the public was able to read the whole story of what was immediately dubbed the "X, Y, Z Affair." The immediate result was an outburst of anti-French feeling which brought the Republican party temporarily to its knees, the nation into an undeclared naval war with France, and a virtual alliance with England and Congress to the enactment of strong defensive measures and domestic legislation which had for its aim the extinction of the opposition party. President Adams became the hero of the moment and the recipient of hundreds of addresses, pledging loyalty and aid in the crisis. Washington shared fully in the anger and could only wonder how, after seeing "that the measure of infamy was filled" and the extent of the "profligacy" and "corruption" of the French government, some Americans could still hold back from condemning it. He believed the leaders of the "Demos" would change their opinions only if a "manifest desertion" from their ranks occurred. Just that seemed to be happening, and in May Hamilton wrote the general, asking if he could not help it along by traveling, ostensibly for his health, through Virginia and North Carolina, and speaking discreetly about the crisis. He also hinted that, if war did break out, Washington was the only possible choice to command the army. The general ingenuously replied that his health had never been better and, more to the point, his presence would not be very persuasive. Politicking was for others, not for him. Soldiering was quite another thing; although he doubted it would come to that, "if a crisis should arrive when a sense of duty, or a call from my Country, should become so imperious as to leave me no choice," he would go, albeit "with as much reluctance from my present peaceful abode, as I should do to the tombs of my Ancestors." Reluctantly, perhaps, but he would accept, and the reluctance may have been more apparent than real as he chose that time to write the president and Secretary McHenry about unrelated matters, almost as if he wanted to call attention to himself.

The precaution, if precaution it was, was unnecessary. In addition to other defensive measures, such as the establishment of a separate Navy Department, Congress had increased the authorized strength of the army by twelve regiments, the "New Army," and the organization of a provisional army, to be called out only in anticipation of an immediate French invasion. It was to the command of the New Army which Washington was likely to be called. Both McHenry and Adams hinted at this, although the president wrote only of asking for the general's name. In answering the Secretary, Washington made clear that he would have to be able to appoint his officers, regardless of the seniority list of the last war. This war, if it came, would bring new conditions, and Washington doubted that, among the veteran officers, one could find "Men of sufficient activity, energy and health, and of *sound politics* [added emph.]" to meet the novel requirements. The military considerations were understandable; a war with the French would be quite different from the War for Independence and Washington surely recalled the difficulties he had during that conflict in securing and keeping competent officers. But the reference to "sound politics" reveals his fears about the ultimate loyalty of some Republicans. In a conflict with the French, perhaps a new type of Loyalist would appear, and the army could not tolerate any of those in its ranks.

Before Washington could be certain his stipulations had been received in Philadelphia, President Adams found it necessary to appoint him to the command without consultation. The general was not the unanimous choice; many Federalists wanted Hamilton to head the proposed force. But the president deeply distrusted him, and just about the last thing he wanted was to see him controlling a real army. Further, Adams saw a navy as the only effective measure against a French invasion; the proposed New Army was important mainly as a negotiating tool, a sign the United States meant business. In order to cut short the pro-Hamilton sentiment, or so he hoped, Adams sent Washington's name to the Senate for approval as lieutenant-general and commander-in-chief of the army; on July 2 the Senate approved the nomination unanimously.

The appointment did not surprise Washington; what concerned him was his inability to set prior conditions; now the conditions would have to be negotiated before acceptance. Hamilton underscored the necessity of this when he warned the general that Adams's military ideas were "of the wrong sort." If Washington accepted the president's appointees for his subordinates, "it will be conceived that the arrangement is yours, and you will be responsible for it in reputation." Hamilton's playing on the older man's concern for his reputation shows not only his knowledge of what arguments carried weight with Washington but also his eagerness to win his point. It was probably unnecessary, as Washington already agreed, and, when McHenry visited Mount Vernon to inform the general of his appointment, he was instructed to write Adams that he would bring back a list of those whom Washington wanted on his staff "and without whom, I think, he would not serve." What followed during the next two months is a very confusing sequence of events which it is impossible to describe here in detail. Washington had stipulated that he would not take the field unless an invasion occurred, so the second-in-command would be in effective charge of the army until then. Under these circumstances, Adams wanted someone he could trust in the second spot. Washington's original choice had been Charles Cotesworth Pinckney, whose residence in South Carolina was advantageous since a French invasion, if it came, was expected in the South. After his visit from McHenry and letters from prominent Federalists, he moved Hamilton forward and placed the New Yorker immediately under him as inspector-general. Adams resisted this as long as he decently could but all the advantages lay with Washington and his still awesome standing with the people; had the conflict turned into a public confrontation, Washington would probably have resigned in protest and American resistance to the French would be weakened along with confidence in the president. Knowing he would lose anyway, Adams dated the commissions for the top three generals, Hamilton, Pinckney, and Henry Knox (who declined to serve under Hamilton, his junior in the war), on the same day, leaving it to Washington to arrange them as he chose and preserving at least the semblance of presidential authority. During the quarrel, Washington used Adams's cabinet as if it were his own, listened to the advice of extreme Federalists only, was conveniently forgetful of statements which could have embarrassed him, and, in the show-down, threatened to take the issue to the public. The affair ended without serious repercussions to the Republic only because John Adams was moderate and George Washington was not. It was one of the sorriest episodes of his adult life.[7]

In late fall, Washington went to the capital to confer with Hamilton and Pinckney over choices from among the flood of applicants for commissions. One of the criteria used turned out to be loyalty to the Federalist party. When Adams tried to appoint two Republicans, Aaron Burr and Frederic Augustus Muhlenberg, brigadier-generals, to help the administration in the key states of New York and Pennsylvania respectively, the generals would not hear of it. Washington had already warned McHenry that the "Brawlers against Government measures" were eager for commissions. "The motives ascribed to them are, that in such a situation they would endeavor to divide, and contaminate the Army, by artful and seditious discourses, and perhaps at a critical moment, bring on confusion." None but the politically pure were to command this army. Washington and Hamilton were also concerned about McHenry's presumed adminis-trative ineptitude so, being unable to remove him, they drew up infinitely detailed regulations and procedures to reduce the likeli-hood of error. All this delayed the organization and enlistment of the New Army past the point where, as will be seen, it was needed. Since President Adams was content to have merely the appearance of additional troops being readied, he ignored New Army affairs, when he was not himself throwing in a monkey wrench of his own.[8]

Although Washington believed himself to be overworked while in the capital, his diary records many more evenings out to dinner than those spent in his lodgings, presumably working. The most bizarre of his evenings out must have when he dined "in a family" with Robert Morris; tactfully omitted from the diary was the place, debtors' prison, where Morris's land speculations had landed him. Washing-ton was not tactful at all when George Logan called, accompanied by a local clergyman. Normally the prominent physician and agricultural reformer would have been a welcome guest, but Dr. Logan was also a Republican who had just returned from a one-man peacemaking effort in France. (His excursion so frightened the Federalists in Congress that they passed a law making such activities illegal; if peacemakers really did inherit the earth, it would only be that part of it under a jail cell.) Despite the physician's persistent attempts to get Washington's attention, the general spoke only to the clergyman until, finally, the latter left. Then Logan tried to reassure Washington that the French had already begun to change their policy, and if the United States refrained from antagonizing them, peace would not be broken. Washington shot back that everything America had done was in self-defense; did the French look

upon us as worms; and not even allowed to turn when tread upon? For it was evident to all the world that we had borne and forborne beyond what even common respect for ourselves required and I hoped that the spirit of this Country would never suffer itself to be injured with impunity by any nation under the Sun.

After replying, the unchastened Logan left. So far had politics taken the man who considered himself above them that he could not listen courteously and dismiss politely a perhaps mistaken but certainly sincere Quaker physician.[9]

At the end of their work, the generals reported on the preparedness of the New Army; in Hamilton's lawyerlike prose, the statement examined the provisions of the law, the existing situation, even the availability of money, and concluded by urging that the force be brought to full strength as soon as possible. All that Washington seems to have contributed to the report was his signature. During the war he had developed the knack of making others' prose his own and had continued this in the presidency; now he was content to let Hamilton speak for him and urge an unwanted army upon an unwilling president.

By early December, Washington, Hamilton, and Pinckney had returned to their homes, leaving McHenry to wrestle as well as he could with the tasks of organizing the New Army and answering respectfully the inquiring, sometimes raspy letters from his generals. Away from the frenetic atmosphere of the capital, war seemed much less likely and Washington soon slackened his demands on McHenry. He was even able to consider calmly, something few other Federalists were, news that President Adams was sending yet another mission to France. In late fall, the president had begun to receive by a variety of channels signals that the French might be ready to treat. Talleyrand had been brought to the decision to change France's American policy by the remarkable success the U.S. Navy had had against French commerce in the Caribbean, the close cooperation between American and English forces and the political successes the undeclared war had given the Federalists. Since the last thing the French wanted was to cement the Federalists, working in a near alliance with the English, in power, a change of policy was in order. Late in 1798 Talleyrand began indirectly (he never did anything directly) to notify Adams of this change; by February 1799, the president was sufficiently convinced of a French willingness to treat to nominate William Vans Murray, already minister to Holland, as minister plenipotentiary to France. Since Talleyrand's signals had been subtle and private, the nation was naturally astonished at the president's action, with one Federalist, Harrison Grey Otis, putting the point succinctly: "Is the man mad?" Washington's initial reaction was also strong; he would have made the French put all their cards on the table before responding formally; as he saw it, the French were "playing the same loose, and roundabout game" as before, but he then admitted that he might not be seeing everything, that "not being acquainted with all the information, and the motives which induced the measure, I may have taken a wrong impression, and therefore shall say nothing further on the subject." As president he had sometimes based decisions on information he could not share with Congress or the people and now he was giving Adams the same leniency he had asked for himself. This may have been induced partly by the fact that Washington himself was one of the channels through which Adams had received his information. Joel Barlow, an American living in Paris, had written the general of the pacific intentions of the French; he had sent the letter on to Adams with the wish that the country might "pass this critical period in an honorable and dignified manner, without being involved in the horrors and calamities of War." Both the general and the nation were recovering from the war fever which had infected them for almost a year.

Congress had reacted to the XYZ dispatches by passing, in addition to defense measures, domestic legislation lumped together under the label, the Alien and Sedition Acts. Even before the news had come from Paris, the Federalists had been upset over the presence of large numbers of French refugees from the Negro rebellion on the island of Santo Domingo, smaller groups of émigrés from metropolitan

France, and some Irish political refugees fleeing the abortive 1798 revolt. These refugees, mixing with American Republicans, seemed to the Federalists to be a direct threat to the integrity of the country. Accordingly Congress made naturalization a lengthier process, gave the president the authority to expel any alien he deemed dangerous, and provided a procedure by which enemy aliens might be removed in event of war. The most important part of this legislation, and the only one to be enforced, was the Sedition Act, which made the common-law crime of seditious libel a matter for prosecution in federal courts. It protected the President, Cabinet, and Congress from criticism and imposed penalties for resisting or opposing the laws of Congress or acts of the President; taken broadly, and it was, it made any criticism of the government a crime. The political intent of the act was obvious from its studied exclusion of the vice-president, Thomas Jefferson, from its protection and in its length, to the end of Adams's administration—March 3, 1801—and no longer. The Sedition Act was a tool to crush the Republican party and to ensure the election of a Federalist (not necessarily Adams) as president in 1800. The act was directed entirely against Republicans, resulting in seventeen convictions, although the level of Federalist political invective was no higher or more factual than that of their opponents; the act was also enforced through prejudiced, partial means, both packed juries and partisan judges being common. It was a reign of legal terror and, while it lasted, it put every Republican editor under the threat of fine and imprisonment. Paradoxically, the effect of the act was to double the number of Republican newspapers in the country.

Although Washington never explicitly approved of the Sedition Act and its companions by name, there is little doubt that he believed them to be necessary and even wholesome pieces of legislation. As early as 1793 he had suggested to Henry Lee that Freneau and Bache's journals had the tendency to bring the government into disrepute, and it was "difficult to prescribe bounds to the effect." In 1794 he linked both the Whiskey Rebellion and the sudden growth of the Democratic-Republican societies to foreign agitation. That same year he vetoed a suggestion of Jefferson's that the president's project of a national university could be easily accomplished by importing the faculty of the University of Geneva, then in danger of being banished by French-inspired revolutionaries. The only immigrants he wanted were useful mechanics and farmers, and even then he did not want them to settle in groups where they would "retain the Language, habits and principles (good and bad) which they bring." After the controversy over Jay's Treaty, the incident which most influenced him toward Federalism, he distrusted immigrants who came here "full of prejudice against their own government, some against all government." And he linked the agitation over the treaty with the activities of French ministers and Republican editors, repeating a favorite Federalist charge.[10]

Shortly after he left the presidency, he commented to Rufus King that nothing would "change the sentiments, or (which perhaps would be more correct) the conduct of some characters amongst us." By the end of 1797 he feared that conduct could include placing the affairs of America under the influence and control of a foreign nation. During the uproar following the publication of the XYZ dispatches, he never expressed any disapproval of any of the government's actions, telling Charles Carroll of Carrollton that "I even wish they had been *more energetic* [orig. emph.]." When Alexander Spotswood doubted the constitutionality and policy of the acts, Washington defended them, although he only argued about the danger of aliens, not dissident citizens. He also defended the acts from John Marshall's criticism of them, commenting that if the Republicans did not have them to criticize, they would find something else. Thus the general tenor of Washington's remarks, at least from the time of the Whiskey Rebellion, shows him gradually adopting the Federalist theory of a Republican plot, possibly initiated but certainly aided by the French, to bring down the government and place the United States under French tutelage. While president, his comments were guarded and indirect and he never proposed any checks on freedom of the press or any other civil liberties; but in retirement he gave full vent, albeit privately, to his fears and suspicions about the Republicans and resident aliens.

As noted, Adams's decision to send yet another mission to France had been hotly resented by the Federalists, and some tried to replace him as candidate in 1800. Washington was naturally high on any list of this kind, and Governor Jonathan Trumbull of Connecticut posed the question forthrightly in July 1799; equally forthrightly, Washington refused. He first suggested that he no longer could give fair value to the public; although he was in good health, "I am not insensible to my declination in other respects." The other reasons showed a grudging recognition of the damage his Federalist politics had done to his reputation; he doubted he would receive one vote from the "Anti-Federal" side, thus any other Federalist could run and do as well as he could, perhaps better. Further, he would be charged "not only with irresolution, but with concealed ambition . . . in short, with dotage and imbecility." When Trumbull persisted, Washington sternly advised him that "principles, instead of men" should be "the steady pursuit of the Federalists." "No eye, no tongue, no thought" should be turned toward his possible candidacy.

Although he refused to take any active part in politics, the general showed a lively interest in national affairs, fretting, for example, at the silence of the French, despite Adams's peace overture. Federalist resistance to Adams's policy had succeeded only in adding two others to serve along with Murray. When the additional representatives left the United States in November 1799, Washington had little faith in their mission: "This business seems to have commenced in an evil hour, and under unfavorable auspices; and I wish mischief may not tread in all its steps, and be the final result of the measure." But since there was nothing he could do about it, he accepted it; as men viewed the same measure differently, he could only hope the President's decision was the correct one.

Although he did not consider himself to be near death—his constant planning for the future of Mount Vernon shows that—in July 1799 Washington took out his best watermarked paper and in his bold, clear hand, and with the utmost attention to neatness and legibility, filled twenty-seven pages with his will. Except for some small bequests, Martha was to have all his property for her lifetime, with the household furnishings, supplies, etc., given outright to her. The Mount Vernon farms were carefully divided, with the larger part and the mansion going to John Augustine's son, Bushrod, and another part to the sons of his late nephew George Augustine. Both his brother and his nephew had managed the estate for him, John during the Virginia Regiment days, George during the early years of the presidency; so in a sense, these were deferred salary payments. Other tracts went to other Washington nephews, and the Western lands were to be sold, the proceeds divided as prescribed among nephews, nieces, and Martha's grandson, George Washington Parke Custis. All specific bequests of land kept it within the Washington family. Any family debts outstanding at the general's death were forgiven. Money bequests and gifts of mementos, swords, and the like were also made to relatives and friends. His secretary, Tobias Lear, received the free life lease of a Mount Vernon farm he was currently renting. In conclusion, he directed his heirs to settle any disputes regarding the will by arbitration, rather than legal process.

In death, as in life, all was to be arranged as much as possible with order and regularity.[11]

Almost as though Providence was compelling the general to contemplate death, news came in September of the final illness of his younger brother Charles, moving him to muse: "I was the *first*, and am now the *last* of my father's children by the second marriage who remain, when I shall be called to follow them, is known only to the giver of life [orig. emph.]." But the "giver" was keeping his intentions to himself, for Washington felt himself to be in fine health as he followed his busy schedule about the farms. One of the few signs of age that showed came when he declined an invitation for himself and Martha to a dancing assembly in Alexandria: "But alas! our dancing days are no more."

On Thursday, December 12, a day marked by rain, sleet, and, finally, snow, Washington made his usual round of the farms on horseback; when he came in, Lear remarked on the snowflakes in his hair but the general brushed them off, saying his greatcoat had kept him dry, and went into dinner immediately, without changing as he usually did. The next day, Washington noted the weather in his diary: "morning snowing and ab[ou]t. 3 inches deep. Wind at the No[rth] E[ast], and Mer[cury] at 30. cont[inuin]g Snowing until 1 O'clock, and Ab[ou]t 4 it became perfectly clear." Despite the cold and snow, as soon as it cleared, he went out on the lawn and marked some trees he wanted taken down, more for the exercise and an opportunity to get out of the house than for any necessity. That evening, although he complained of a sore throat and sounded hoarse, he sat with Martha and Lear, reading newspapers and frequently commenting on interesting or humorous items with no serious discomfort apparent.

In the middle of the night, however, he woke Martha, complaining of an extremely sore throat and difficulty in breathing. With the dawn, of the 14th, Lear and one of the overseers were sent for, the overseer to bleed the general at his own insistence, for he believed it to be the sovereign remedy for all ills. Lear tried to get him to swallow a soothing mixture but he could not get it down and the secretary contented himself with bathing the throat externally; despite Lear's gentleness, Washington complained, " 'Tis very sore." During the morning Dr. Craik, his friend since the days of the Virginia Regiment, came to bleed him again; he also tried to get the patient to swallow a palliative, but again he could not swallow it and Craik noted he was having increasing trouble breathing. That afternoon Craik was joined by Doctors Elisha Cullen Dick and Gustavus Richard Brown.

Nothing they prescribed, which included doses of emetics and laxatives, blisters, and two more bleedings, eased Washington's breathing or lessened the pain. Dr. Dick, the youngest of the physicians, proposed a novel treatment, a tracheotomy to permit the general to breathe, but this was vetoed by the older men as too untried and drastic.[12]

Washington bore with the various treatments patiently until early evening, when he whispered to the physicians: "I feel myself going, I thank you for your attentions; but I pray you to take no more trouble about me, let me go off quietly, I can not last long." Earlier he had given Lear some brief directions about his papers, confided to him his belief that he would not survive this illness, and thanked him for his attempts to make him comfortable. After his directions to the physicians, he did not speak again until about ten o'clock, when he motioned Lear close to him. Lear reported that

he made several attempts to speak to me before he could effect it, at length he said,—"I am just going. Have me decently buried; and do not let my body be put into the Vault in less than three days after I am dead." I bowed assent, for I could not speak. He then looked at me again and said, "Do you understand me?" I replied "Yes." "'Tis well," said he.

He spoke no other words; twenty minutes later he died. Lear wrote that, throughout the long and painful day, Washington had borne his illness with "patience, fortitude, & resignation . . . always endeavouring (from a sense of duty as it appeared) to take what was offered him, and to do as he was desired by the Physicians." His sense of duty, hard earned but well learned, stayed with him to the last.[13]

CHAPTER 8

Ordinary Man, Extraordinary Leader

Simple truth is his best, his greatest eulogy.
She alone can render his fame immortal.
—Abigail Adams

MRS. Adams's advice is well worth pondering by anyone who is attempting to arrive at a proper appreciation of a great man, but especially so in the case of Washington, about whom the words were written. Perhaps that perceptive lady realized the extent to which Americans would obscure the simple truth with both adoring myth and debunking billingsgate until the outline of the historical Washington was lost. Not that the mythologizing and its almost inevitable sequel, debunking, are alone responsible for making Washington a difficult person to understand. Any one of us is sufficiently complex to challenge the skills of the biographer and that complexity is magnified when a person moves through an era as consequential as the American Revolution. All that the misrepresentation of Washington has done is to increase the difficulties of an already formidable undertaking, the writing of another's life. What follows is my personal distillation of the most significant accomplishments and the essential personality of George Washington.

W. E. Woodward has commented that Washington was an ordinary man raised to the highest levels; although he meant that comment to be disparaging, it has always struck me as one of the most telling compliments anyone could have paid the Father of his Country. His talents in most fields were relatively commonplace; what he did was to raise those talents to the level of superlative accomplishment by self-discipline, a character trait in which he was certainly extraordinary. This enabled him, in turn, to pay unremitting attention to details, essential to coordinating all the disparate parts of an organization so they worked toward the accomplishment of a goal, whether it be the lands and slaves of Mount Vernon toward the attaining of personal wealth or the resources of the States and the

157

soldiers of the Continental Army toward a victory over the English. Helping him in this was an innate liking for symmetry and order and an aptitude—more aptly, perhaps, a fascination—for counting and computation. But these gifts, like those of truly ordinary men, would have been ineffectual without his self-discipline and devotion to duty; how many of us ordinary men make such effective use of our natural talents? Few, because few of us are willing to work as hard as Washington did.

Aside from his discipline and devotion to duty—with Washington, two sides of the same coin, practically speaking—it is difficult to single out any commanding characteristics; a nineteenth-century English writer put it well: "the imposing effect [of Washington] is more dependent upon the nice balance and exact symmetry of parts, than upon the commanding stature of any of his faculties, if estimated singly."[1] But those nicely balanced components can be commented on separately.

One of the first things to be noted is that, as an adult, Washington was very different from what he was as a youth; there was a steady maturing which refined out much that was gross and unpleasant and left behind a highly controlled personality which constantly disciplined the very strong feelings and almost uncontrollable impulses of the young Washington. Since the early death of his father had deprived him of the inheritance and help necessary to place him securely in Virginia society, he looked to his step-brothers for the "interest" he needed. Lawrence supplied it both by his own efforts and his introduction of the young boy to the Fairfaxes; the early commissions from Governor Dinwiddie owed a good bit to Fairfax friendship. As a young man, Washington was also strongly acquisitive; witness his concern over his salary and his efforts to get Dinwiddie to increase it. In his attempt to get a royal commission, he curried favor with both Braddock and Forbes as well as Lord Loudoun; commissions were commonly recommended only for favorites, and he did much to be a favorite. Yet he was also a most difficult subordinate for Governor Dinwiddie, constantly demanding more of everything with no realization of the difficulties under which the older man was working. Although he could forget his own concerns, as when he antagonized Forbes by his relentless championing of Virginia's interest in Braddock's road, he generally kept them to the fore, as when he pushed through the redemption of the 1754 land bounty, thus securing more than 30,000 acres on the Ohio, although the bonus was probably meant only for the enlisted men.

As Washington established himself at Mount Vernon, he became more relaxed about acquiring land, although he never lost his interest in what he saw as the most secure of all assets. And it ought to be noted that his personal honesty was never questioned and he had a reputation for integrity as good as any man's. But the most significant development of the 1760s was one which was not obvious until he assumed command of the Continental Army, and that was the iron self-control he had succeeded in imposing on himself. General Washington could not be said to be a perfect example of calmness and serenity; he gave way to fits of temper and he often tended to view his immediate situation in the gloomiest way possible, yet the contrast between the Colonel and the General is striking and unmistakable; he immersed himself in the cause of American independence with a singular lack of regard for his person and fortune and became a symbol of America's unswerving desire to be free of English dominance.

What came to the fore so noticeably during the war was Washington's practice of the Stoic ideal that the favor of a free people was the highest reward a citizen could receive. Thus his service for expenses only was not a theatrical gesture but rather a practical example of his belief that public approval was the only proper coin for public service. This was not an unalloyed benefit. Although it permitted him to act unselfishly with regard to money, it also made him very sensitive of his reputation and difficult for him to accept criticism. Washington often professed a willingness to listen to serious, fair criticism, but comment by anyone outside the army was usually put down as uninformed. Criticism from inside the army was seen as a plot to unseat him: for example, the Conway Cabal.

His sensitivity about his reputation sometimes made it difficult for him to make up his mind as he tried to puzzle out the effect different steps might have on his standing with the people but this is hard to assess separately for he was always slow in coming to a conclusion. This was partly because he realized that many of his actions might have a long-term significance; this was frequently stated, even when he was in the army, but especially so when he was serving as president. Thomas Jefferson once said that Washington's mind was "slow in operation, being little aided by invention or imagination, but sure in conclusion."[2] Early in his career, he had developed the habit of asking anyone suitable for advice, then making up his mind and giving his decision only at the last minute. Slow in coming to a decision, he was quick and unrelenting in execution. As president, this worked admirably, for most problems were long-term and, in that more leisurely age, crises took their time in developing. This slow deliberation also held back Washington's tendency to move quickly, an impetuosity more characteristic of the gambler than the statesman but a side he did possess. Asking everyone for advice, however, helped to lead to the frequent charges that he was unduly influenced by those around him, such charges usually coming from those whose advice was not accepted.

One aspect of Washington's personality which impressed contemporaries was his silence, which, the more perceptive noted, concealed his control of strong feelings. As John Adams commented, perhaps enviously, Washington possessed the "gift of silence. . . . He had great self command. It cost him a great exertion sometimes, and a constant constraint; but to preserve so much equaminity as he did required a great capacity." Washington himself realized this, for he once said he had tried to do his duty "as far as human frailties and perhaps strong passions" allowed him.[3]

The strong feelings to which both Washington and Adams referred included a strong streak of pessimism lying just below the surface of Washington's apparently calm exterior. The need to keep this and his other feelings under control helps to explain the almost ceaseless activity in which he immersed himself: work, exercise—either horseback-riding or, in the worst weather, pacing the Mount Vernon veranda—the preoccupation with detail, even to the point of calculating the number of seeds in a pound of timothy or rye seed and counting the number of panes of glass in the mansion house at Mount Vernon. As long as he had something to do, the furies could be kept at bay.

Despite his silence and gravity, he was able to capture and hold the affections of those near him, especially the younger men who served on his staff during the war. This was true even in the days of the Virginia Regiment, as his officers testified in a moving statement when he resigned his commission in December 1758. But he was respected, not loved, by the enlisted men and his General Orders to them were rigid and admonishing; in Marcus Cunliffe's words: "They do not give praise; they bestow it."

Washington's generalship, his role in the formation of the Constitution, and his conduct of the presidency have already been discussed. Here I would like simply to underline the essentially symbolic role which he played in each of these areas; this is not to denigrate his accomplishments, but while other men could have been adequate generals, presided over the Convention, and seen the new government into being, it is hard to see anyone other than Washington holding the army and then the states together as he did. In becoming the symbol of the unity of the colonies by serving as commander-in-chief of the army, he assumed a role which he thereafter found impossible to forsake. His lapse into partisanship in the last years of his administration did not seriously tarnish his image with other than partisan Republicans in Congress, for once Jay's Treaty was ratified his other actions could be explained by the necessity of executing the treaty. France's subsequent reaction to the disadvantages Jay's Treaty had placed her under was laid at John Adams's door. Furthermore, most Americans were not yet involved in the discord between Federalist and Republican and ignored the allegations of the latter regarding Washington's activities. The partisan selection of the officer corps of the New Army during the Quasi War did not become generally known and, since the army was not actually raised, was of little practical significance. Thus, for most Americans, Washington was never identified with either political party. He remained, in Henry Lee's now hackneyed but still accurate phrase, "First in war, first in peace, first in the hearts of his countrymen."

Washington gave the United States what history has demonstrated every new nation needs, a leader who stands above the contention of the moment and ties the disparate parts of the country together until a national spirit has developed, but he did this, as few others have, without giving serious ground for fearing the introduction of monarchical or authoritarian rule. No one has said it quite as well as Thomas Jefferson:

His was the singular destiny and merit of leading the armies of his country successfully through an arduous war for the establishment of its independence, of conducting its councils through the birth of a government, new in its forms and principles, until it settled down into a quiet and orderly train; and of scrupulously obeying the laws through the whole of his career, civil and military, of which the history of the world furnishes no other example.[4]

That was Washington's most significant contribution to the success of the American Revolution.

Notes and References

Chapter One

1. D. S. Freeman, *George Washington*, I (New York: Scribner's, 1948), pp. 17–47 and Chap. V.

2. Charles Moore, ed., *George Washington's Rules of Civility* (Boston: Houghton, Mifflin, 1926), pp. xiv, 5–21.

3. Freeman, GW, I, xix, 192–95, 198–99.

4. S. E. Morison, "Young Man Washington," *By Land and By Sea* (New York: Knopf, 1953), pp. 168–72; M. Cunliffe, *George Washington* (1958, rpt. New York: New American Library, n.d.), pp. 162–63.

5. J. C. Fitzpatrick, ed., *The Diaries of George Washington*, I (Boston: Houghton, Mifflin, 1925), pp. 1–17; as the *Diaries* are arranged chronologically, reference hereafter will only be made to special entries.

6. GW to Wm. Fauntleroy, Sr., May 20, 1753, J. C. Fitzpatrick, ed., *The Writings of George Washington*, I (Washington: GPO, 1931), p. 22; see also p. 19; as GW's letters, General Orders, circular letters while general, speeches while president, etc., are arranged chronologically, reference hereafter will be made only where I am using a letter different in time from the text or a special entry.

7. *Diaries*, I, 41–67; J. R. Alden, *Robert Dinwiddie* (Williamsburg, Va.: Col. Williamsburg, 1973).

8. R. Dinwiddie to GW, [Mar. 1754], R. A. Brock, ed., "The Official Records of Robert Dinwiddie," *Coll. of Virginia Hist. Soc.*, III (1889), 59; see *Writings*, I, 31–104 for GW's reports.

9. F. Tilberg, "Washington's Stockade at Fort Necessity," *Pa. Hist.*, XX (1953), 240–57.

10. See G. F. Leduc, *Washington and "the Murder of Jumonville"* (Boston: Franco-Amer. Hist. Soc., 1933), for a full treatment; Freeman, GW, I, 402–12.

11. Freeman, GW, I, Chap. V; see C. I. A. Ritchie, ed., *Braddock's Expedition* (London: n.p., 1962) and E. Hamilton, ed., *Braddock's Defeat* (Norman: Univ. of Oklahoma Press, 1959), for relevant documents.

12. "Biographical Memoranda," [Oct. 1786], *Writings*, XXIX, 46.

13. N. Anderson, "The General Chooses a Road—The Forbes Campaign of 1758 to Capture Fort Duquesne," *W. Pa. Hist. Mag.* 42 (1959), 109–38, 241–58, 383–401.

Chapter Two

1. J. T. Flexner, *George Washington*, I (Boston: Little, Brown, 1965), pp. 196–205, includes the text of the recently recovered original; Morison, *Land & Sea*, p. 178.

2. G. Mercer in W. S. Baker, ed., *Early Sketches of George Washington* (Philadelphia: Lippincott, 1894), pp. 13–14.

3. Flexner, GW, I, 286.

4. P. Wilstach, *Mount Vernon* (Garden City, N.Y.: Doubleday, 1925), p. 134; *Diaries*, I, 246n.

5. P. F. Boller, Jr., *George Washington and Religion* (Dallas: Southern Methodist Univ. Press, 1963), p. 27; Wilstach, *Mt. Vernon*, pp. 106–107.

6. P. L. Haworth, *George Washington, Country Gentleman* (Indianapolis: Bobbs-Merrill, 1925), pp. 68, 71–72, 92–93; *Diaries*, I, 153–54, 158.

7. Ray B. Cook, *Washington's Western Lands* (Strasburg, Va.: Shenandoah Publ. House, 1930), p. 2; B. Knollenberg, *George Washington: The Virginia Period, 1732–1775* (Durham, N.C.: Duke Univ. Press, 1964), pp. 91 ff.

8. G. L. Nute, "Washington and the Potomac, 1769–1796," *Am. Hist. Rev.*, XXVII (1922–23), 497–519, 705–727.

9. C. S. Sydnor, *Gentlemen Freeholders: Political Practices in Washington's Virginia* (Chapel Hill, N.C.: Univ. of North Carolina Press, 1952), pp. 68–79; Louise Griffith, *The Virginia House of Burgesses*, rev. ed. (University, Ala.: Univ. of Alabama Press, 1970), pp. 58–60, 143; Jack P. Greene, *The Quest for Power* (1962, rpt. New York: Norton, 1972), p. 274.

10. R. L. Scribner, ed., *Revolutionary Virginia: The Road to Independence*, I (Charlottesville, Va.: Univ. Press of Virginia, 1973), has the relevant documents; A. M. Schlesinger, *The Colonial Merchants and the American Revolution* (1917, rpt. New York: Ungar, 1957), pp. 135–38, 197–99, 236; B. W. Labaree, *The Boston Tea Party* (New York: Oxford, 1964), Chaps. IV, V; see L. H. Gipson, *The Coming of the Revolution 1763–1775* (New York: Harper, 1954), for a general treatment of the period.

11. E. C. Burnett, *The Continental Congress* (1941, rpt. New York: Norton, 1964), Chaps. II, III; S. Deane to Mrs. Deane, Sep. 10, 1774, E. C. Burnett, ed., *Letters of Members of the Continental Congress*, I (1921, rpt. Gloucester, Mass.: Peter Smith, 1963), pp. 28–29; Flexner, GW, I, 327.

12. O. W. Spaulding, "The Military Studies of George Washington," *Am. Hist. Rev.*, XXIX (1923–24), 678.

Chapter Three

1. Scribner, ed., *Revolutionary Virginia*, I, and Burnett, *Congress* and *Letters* remain useful; Flexner, GW, I, 328n. for the verse; see J. R. Alden,

The American Revolution, 1775–1783 (New York: Harper, 1954) for a general treatment of the period.

2. Knollenberg, *GW: Virginia*, Chap. 17.

3. Christopher Ward, *The War of the Revolution*, J. R. Alden, ed., 2 vols (New York: Macmillan, 1952) and Don C. Higginbotham, *The War of American Independence: Military Attitudes, Policies and Practice, 1763–1789* (New York: Macmillan, 1971) are excellent military histories; C. H. Lesser, ed., *The Sinews of Independence: Monthly Strength Reports of the Continental Army* (Chicago: Univ. of Chicago Press, 1976); R. B. Morris and H. S. Commager, eds., *The Spirit of Seventy-Six*, 2 vols. (Indianapolis: Bobbs-Merrill, 1958), for invaluable primary documents and bibliography.

4. C. Nettels, *George Washington and American Independence* (Boston: Little, Brown, 1951), for GW's contribution in this area.

5. Flexner, GW, II, Chap. XI for a judicious assessment of GW's generalship; see G. A. Billias, ed., *George Washington's Generals* (New York: Morrow, 1964) and same, *George Washington's Opponents* (New York: Morrow, 1969), for evaluations of the principal commanders on both sides.

6. B. Knollenberg, *George Washington and the Revolution* (1940, rpt. New York: Archon, 1968), Chap. XII for GW's thoughts on bounties, etc.

7. Bruce Bliven, Jr., *Battle for Manhattan* (1956, rpt. Baltimore: Pelican, 1964), is a good, popular account of the campaign.

8. C. F. Adams, *Studies Military and Diplomatic* (New York: Macmillan, 1911), Chaps. II and III, are good discussions of the Battle of Long Island.

9. Knollenberg, *Washington and the Revolution*, pp. 132–38.

10. J. R. Alden, *General Charles Lee: Traitor or Patriot?* (Baton Rouge: Louisiana St. Univ. Press, 1951), pp. 145–55; and J. F. Roche, *Joseph Reed* (1957, rpt. New York: AMS Press, 1968), pp. 98–103, for the two principals in this episode; "Lee Papers," *New-York Hist. Soc. Colls.*, II (1872), 89–341, for Lee's letters; L. Lundin, *Cockpit of the Revolution: The War for Independence in New Jersey* (Princeton: Princeton Univ. Press, 1940) and W. S. Stryker, *The Battles of Trenton and Princeton* (Boston: Houghton, Mifflin, 1898), for the fighting of Dec. 1776–Jan. 1777.

11. Ward, *War*, I, Chaps. 30, 31; Freeman, GW, IV, 488; see Adams, *Studies*, Chap. IV for a negative assessment of GW's generalship; J. S. Pancake, *1777: The Year of the Hangman* (University, Ala.: Univ. of Alabama Press, 1977), Chap. XI justifies GW's conduct.

12. Pancake, *1777*, Chap. XIII, for the river forts; Ward, *War*, I, Chap. 33, for the Battle of Germantown.

13. A. H. Bill, *Valley Forge: The Making of an Army* (New York: Harper, 1952); L. C. Hatch, *The Administration of the American Revolutionary Army* (New York: Longmans, Green, 1904), p. 122.

14. I prefer Knollenberg, *Washington and the Revolution*, Chaps. V–VIII, for this episode, but see also Freeman, GW, IV, Chaps. 20–25; Flexner, GW, II, Chaps. 27–30; Higginbotham, *War*, Chap. 9 and J. G. Rossie, *The Politics*

of Command in the American Revolution (Syracuse, N.Y.: Syracuse Univ. Press, 1975), Chap. XIII.

15. J. M. Palmer, *General Von Steuben* (New Haven: Yale Univ. Press, 1937), pp. 114–16, 129, 160–61; Ward, *War*, II, 554.

16. W. S. Stryker, *The Battle of Monmouth* (Princeton: Princeton Univ. Press, 1927) describes the battle in detail and reprints relevant documents; see Alden, *Lee*, Chaps. XIV–XVI, for a fair presentation of Lee's side of what followed: "Lee Papers," *New-York Hist. Soc. Colls.*, III (1873) and IV (1874) for Lee's letters.

17. Carl Van Doren, *Secret History of the American Revolution* (New York: Viking, 1941); Chaps. 6–15 treat Arnold's treason exhaustively.

18. Carl Van Doren, *Mutiny in January* (New York: Viking, 1948) is a full recounting; see I. Shreve to GW, Jan. 20, 1781, *Writings*, XXI, 124n.; Freeman, GW, V, 245–50.

19. B. Mitchell, "Hamilton's Quarrel with Washington," *Wm. and Mary Qly.*, 3s., XII (1955), 199–216.

20. Thomas J. Fleming, *Beat the Last Drum* (New York: St. Martin's, 1963) is a good, popular account of Yorktown; Freeman, GW, V, Chaps. XXI–XXIII, details GW's role.

21. Piers Mackesy, *The War for America, 1775–1783* (Cambridge, Mass.: Harvard Univ. Press, 1964), pp. 435–36.

22. Hatch, *Administration*, p. 147; Allen Bowman, *The Morale of the American Revolutionary Army* (Washington: Amer. Council on Public Affairs, 1943), p. 24; R. H. Kohn, "The Inside History of the Newburgh Conspiracy: America and the Coup d'Etat," *Wm. and Mary Qly.*, 3s., XXVII (1970), 187–220; and the same author's slightly different treatment in *Eagle and Sword* (New York: Free Press, 1975), Chap. 2.

Chapter Four

1. Haworth, GW, pp. 286–88, 52–53, 116–17, 120–28, 66–67, 107–10; Wilstach, *Mount Vernon*, pp. 151–52.

2. P. L. Ford, *The True George Washington* (Philadelphia: Lippincott, 1898), p. 150; Haworth, GW, pp. 193–209; W. B. Mazyck, *George Washington and the Negro* (Washington: Associated Publishers, 1932), p. 98.

3. Boller, *GW and Religion*, pp. 46,64,108; J. R. Alden, *The South in the Revolution* (Baton Rouge: Louisiana St. Univ. Press, 1957), p. 321.

4. C. Bacon-Foster, "Early Chapters in the Development of the Potomac Route to the West," *Rec. of the Columbia Hist. Soc.*, 15 (1912), 96–322.

5. Many writers have treated the events leading to the Phila. Convention; my favorite is Clinton Rossiter, *1787: The Grand Convention* (1966, rpt. New York: New American Library, 1968); C. C. Tansill, ed., *Documents Illustrative of the Formation of the Union of American States* (Washington: GPO, 1927), is an excellent collection of documents, including a generous

portion of James Madison's notes of the Convention's proceedings; "Federalists" and "Antifederalists" will be used to indicate the supporters and opponents, respectively, of the movement to strengthen the central govt.

6. A. N. Holcombe, "The Role of Washington in the Framing of the Constitution," *Huntington Library Qly.*, XIX (1955–56), 317–34; H. W. Bradley, "The Political Thinking of George Washington," *Jour. of Southern History*, XI (1945), 469–86.

Chapter Five

1. Freeman, GW, VI, Chap. VII, for the journey to New York; see J. C. Miller, *The Federalist Era, 1789–1801* (New York: Harper, 1960), for the general history of the period.

2. T. E. V. Smith, *The City of New York in the Year of Washington's Inauguration, 1789* (New York: Randolph, 1889), Chap. VII.

3. E. S. Maclay, ed., *The Journal of William Maclay* (1890, rpt. New York: Ungar, 1965), p. 9.

4. *Ibid.*, pp. 20–37, for GW's title; p. 67 for levees; pp. 134–35 for dinners; A. Adams to M. Cranch, Jan. 5, 1790, S. Mitchell, ed., *New Letters of Abigail Adams, 1788–1801* (Boston: Houghton, Mifflin, 1947), p. 35.

5. S. Decatur, Jr., *The Private Affairs of George Washington* (Boston: Houghton, Mifflin, 1933), pp. xi, 12–13, 49, 101, 108–109, 118, 156–57, 329–30.

6. Haworth, GW, pp. 246–47; T. Jefferson to J. Madison, Jun. 4, 1793, P. L. Ford, ed., *The Writings of Thomas Jefferson*, VI (New York: Putnam's, 1895), p. 293; see Rufus Griswold, *The Republican Court, or American Society in the Days of Washington* (New York: Appleton, 1854), pp. 365–71, for more examples of this.

7. G. Hunt, "Office Seeking during Washington's Administration," *Am. Hist. Rev.*, I (1896), 270–83.

8. T. Jefferson to heads of depts., Nov. 6, 1801 in Leonard White, *The Federalists: A Study in Administrative History, 1789–1801* (1948, rpt. New York: Free Press, 1965), p. 35; GW to Comte de Moustier, May 25, 1789 in *ibid.*, p. 31; see also Chaps. I, III and IX.

9. "Madison's Personal Memoranda," May 5, 1792, V. H. Paltsits, ed., *Washington's Farewell Message* (New York: New York Public Library, 1935), pp. 11–13, 212–17.

10. Jefferson's and Hamilton's arguments are in, respectively, Dumas Malone, *Thomas Jefferson*, II (Boston: Little, Brown, 1951), Chap. XX; and B. Mitchell, *Alexander Hamilton*, II (New York: Macmillan, 1962), Chap. 5.

11. Maclay, *Diary*, pp. 125–28; see R. J. Dangerfield, *In Defense of the Senate: A Study in Treaty Making* (1933, rpt. Port Washington, N.Y.: Kennikat, 1966), pp. 41–49, for a fuller treatment.

12. E. James Ferguson, *The Power of the Purse: A History of American Public Finance* (Chapel Hill: Univ. of North Carolina Press, 1961), Chaps. 13–15, for a sure guide through the funding controversy.

13. Maclay, *Diary*, pp. 304, 319.

14. See the sources cited in n. 10, above.

15. F. B. Sawvel, ed., *The Anas of Thomas Jefferson* (1903, rpt. New York: DaCapo, 1970), pp. 29–30, 36.

16. W. B. Bryan, *A History of the National Capital* (New York: Macmillan, 1904), I; L. D. Scisco, "A Site for the 'Federal City': the Original Proprietors and the Negotiations with Washington," *Rec. of the Columbia Hist. Soc.* (1957–59), pp. 123–47.

17. Sawvel, ed., *Jefferson Anas*, pp. 51–52.

18. Ibid., p. 84.

19. Freeman, GW, VI, 364–71, cites all the relevant letters.

20. Sawvel, ed., *Jefferson Anas*, pp. 103–105; see M. D. Conway's introduction to a collection of GW's letters to Whiting's successor, Wm. Pearce, *Memoirs of the Long Island Hist. Soc.*, IV (1889).

Chapter Six

1. See W. N. Chambers, *Political Parties in a New Nation* (New York: Oxford, 1963); Joseph Charles, *The Origins of the American Party System* (1956, rpt. New York: Harper, 1961); N. E. Cunningham, Jr., *The Jeffersonian Republicans: The Formation of Party Organization, 1789–1801* (Chapel Hill: Univ. of North Carolina Press, 1957), for general treatments of party development; L. M. Sears, *George Washington & the French Revolution* (Detroit: Wayne St. Univ. Press, 1960), is a competent survey of the subject.

2. See C. R. Ritcheson, *Aftermath of Revolution: British Policy toward the United States, 1783–1795* (1969, rpt. New York: Norton, 1971); Bradford Perkins, *The First Rapprochement: England and the United States, 1795–1805* (Berkeley: Univ. of California Press, 1967); J. A. James, "French Diplomacy and American Politics, 1794–95," *Annual Rep.* of the Am. Hist. Assoc. (1913), I, 151–63; E. W. Lyon, "The Directory and the United States," *Am. Hist. Rev.*, XLIII (1937–38), 514–32; F. J. Turner, "The Policy of France toward the Mississippi Valley in the Period of Washington and Adams," *Am. Hist. Rev.*, X (1904–1905), 249–79, for the diplomatic background.

3. Sawvel, ed., *Jefferson Anas*, p. 116.

4. Charles M. Thomas, *American Neutrality in 1793* (New York: Columbia Univ. Press, 1931), p. 28, is also important for its analysis of the evolution of American neutral policy; Sawvel, ed., *Jefferson Anas*, pp. 118–19.

5. John J. Reardon, *Edmund Randolph* (New York: Macmillan, 1974), p. 222.

6. H. Ammon, *The Genet Mission* (New York: Norton, 1973) is an excellent study of Genet's work and its domestic repercussions.

7. T. Jefferson to J. Madison, May 19, Jul. 7, 1793, *Jefferson Writings*, VI, 259–62, 338–39.

8. Sawvel, ed., *Jefferson Anas*, pp. 153–66.

9. Eugene P. Link, *The Democratic-Republican Societies, 1790–1800* (1942, rpt. New York: Octagon, 1965), is the standard work on the societies.

10. S. F. Bemis, *Jay's Treaty*, rev. ed. (New Haven: Yale Univ. Press, 1960) treats the negotiation in detail; Charles, *Origins*, Chap. III, gives the political background from a pro-Republican point of view.

11. Leland D. Baldwin, *Whiskey Rebels*, rev. ed. (Pittsburgh: Univ. of Pittsburgh Press, 1968), Chap. I, for a description of the pioneers' sentiments.

12. Kohn, *Eagle and Sword*, Chap. 8, analyzes well the administration's decision-making process; the Rebellion is described adequately here and in Baldwin, *Rebels*.

13. See Reardon, *Randolph*, Chaps. 16–19; see also the older study of M. D. Conway, *Omitted Chapters of History Disclosed in the Life and Papers of Edmund Randolph* (New York: Putnam's, 1888) for its extensive quotations of documents.

14. W. C. Ford, ed., "Edmund Randolph on the British Treaty, 1795," *Am. Hist. Rev.*, XII (1906–1907), 587–99; the only record of GW's reaction is in [Edmund Randolph,] *A Vindication of Mr. Randolph's Resignation* (Philadelphia: Samuel H. Smith, 1795), pp. 30–32.

15. E. Randolph to GW, Jul. 31, 1795, 274 GW Papers, 39, Lib. Cong.; T. Pickering to GW, Jul. 31, 1795, O. Pickering and C. W. Upham, *The Life of Timothy Pickering*, III (Boston: Little, Brown, 1873), pp. 188–89.

16. O. Wolcott, "Notes Relative to Fauchet's Letter," George Gibbs, *Memoirs of the Administrations of Washington and Adams, Edited from the Papers of Oliver Wolcott* (New York: Van Norden, 1846), p. 232; see also ibid., pp. 232–56; T. Pickering, "Miscellaneous Notes, [1826]," Pickering and Upham, *Pickering*, III, 216–19.

17. Based on Randolph's *Vindication* and the Pickering and Wolcott material cited above.

18. Reardon, *Randolph*, p. 333; see I. Brant, "Edmund Randolph, Not Guilty!", *Wm. and Mary Qly.*, 3s., VII (1950), 179–198, for a modern vindication of Randolph.

19. J. Adams to A. Adams, Feb. 8, 1796, C. F. Adams, ed., *Letters of John Adams Addressed to His Wife*, II (Boston: Little, Brown, [1841]), p. 195.

20. D. H. Stewart, *The Opposition Press of the Federalist Period* (Albany: St. Univ. of New York Press, 1969), pp. 520–31.

21. S. F. Bemis, *Pinckney's Treaty*, rev. ed. (New Haven: Yale Univ. Press, 1960).

22. Paltsits, ed., *Farewell Message*, describes and documents the process of composition.

23. A. DeConde, "Washington's Farewell, the French Alliance and the Election of 1796," *Miss. Vlly. Hist. Rev.*, XLIII (1957), 641–58; reprinted,

along with other, contrasting, treatments in B. I. Kaufman, ed., *Washington's Farewell Address* (Chicago: Quadrangle, 1969).

24. The *Boston Gazette* is quoted from Paltsits, ed., *Farewell Message*, p. 63; other reactions are on pp. 59–74.

25. G. H. Clarfield, *Timothy Pickering and American Diplomacy, 1795–1800* (Columbia: Univ. of Missouri Press, 1969), pp. 61–65.

26. B. W. Bond, Jr., "The Monroe Mission to France, 1794–1796," *Johns Hopkins Univ. Studies in History and Pol. Sci.*, Ser. XXV, Nos. 2–3 (Feb.–Mar. 1907); H. Ammon, *James Monroe* (New York: McGraw-Hill, 1971), pp. 108–56.

27. H. Liston to J. Jackson, Dec. 9, 1796, B. Perkins, ed., "A Diplomat's Wife in Philadelphia: Letters of Henrietta Liston, 1796–1800," *Wm. and Mary Qly.*, 3s., XI (1954), 606; J. C. Nicholls, ed., "Lady Henrietta Liston's Journal of Washington's 'Resignation,' Retirement, and Death," *Pa. Mag. of Hist. and Biog.*, XCV (1971), 516.

28. "Letter to George Washington, July 30, 1796," P. S. Foner, ed., *The Complete Writings of Thomas Paine* (New York: Citadel, 1945), II, 691–723; *Aurora*, Mar. 5, 1797, quoted in Stewart, *Opposition Press*, p. 534; H. Liston to J. Jackson, Oct. 16, 1796, *Wm. and Mary Qly.*, 3s., XI (1954), 604.

29. J. Adams to A. Adams, Mar. 5, 1797, *Adams Letters to Wife*, 244.

Chapter Seven

1. GW to T. Lear, Mar. 9, 1797, *Letters and Recollections of George Washington: Being letters to Tobias Lear . . .* (New York: Doubleday, Page & Co., 1906), pp. 114–16.

2. Flexner, GW, IV, Chap. 12, describes GW's thoughts and plans.

3. H. Liston to J. Jackson, Dec. 8, 1797, *Wm. and Mary Qly.*, 3s., XI (1954), 614.

4. GW to E. Powel, Mar. 26, 1797, in J. A. Carroll and M. W. Ashworth, *George Washington*, VII (New York: Scribner's, 1957; completing the biography by D. S. Freeman), 449.

5. James Monroe, *View of the Conduct of the Executive in the Foreign Affairs of the United States Connected with the Mission to the French Republic, 1794, 5 & 6* (Philadelphia: B. F. Bache, 1797); GW's comments, along with the relevant passages from Monroe, are in *Writings*, XXXVI, 194–237.

6. My description of the XYZ Affair and its repercussions is based on A. DeConde, *The Quasi-War: The Politics and Diplomacy of the Undeclared War with France, 1797–1801* (New York: Scribner's, 1966), Chaps. II, III; S. G. Kurtz, *The Presidency of John Adams* (Philadelphia: Univ. of Pennsylvania Press, 1957), Chap. 13.

7. This brief account is based on Carroll and Ashworth, GW, VII, 510 ff.; Flexner, GW, IV, Chaps. 40, 41; Kohn, *Eagle and Sword*, Chap. 11; and the relevant correspondence in *Writings*, XXXVII.

8. J. Adams to R. Rush, Aug. 11, 1813, quoted in Kurtz, *Adams Presidency*, p. 329; Kohn, *Eagle and Sword*, Chap. 12; see M. Smelser, "George Washington and the Alien and Sedition Acts," *Am. Hist. Rev.*, LIX (1953–54), 333, for documentation on GW's insistence on "sound politics."

9. "Memorandum of an Interview [with George Logan]," Tue., Nov. 13, 1798, *Writings*, XXXVII, 18–20.

10. Smelser, *Am. Hist. Rev.*, LIX (1953–54), 322–34, describes GW's reaction to this legislation; James M. Smith, *Freedom's Fetters* (Ithaca, N.Y.: Cornell Univ. Press, 1956), is an excellent study of the law and politics of the Acts.

11. The will and GW's "Schedule of Property" are in *Writings*, XXXVII, 275–303.

12. This account is based on Tobias Lear's "The last illness and death of General Washington," *Letters . . . of George Washington*, pp. 129–41.

13. There has been a good bit of controversy over the medical treatment received by Washington during his last illness; see Carrol and Ashworth, GW, VII, App. VII–2. Drs. Craik, Brown, and Dick should not be censured; their diagnosis and treatment were thoroughly in accord with the best contemporary medical practice. It was the state of medical knowledge that was deficient, not its practitioners. A modern evaluation of Washington's illness would describe it as a throat inflammation, perhaps of bacterial or viral origin, which caused swelling of the larynx severe enough to choke off the patient's breath.

Chapter Eight

1. Cyrus Edwards in Baker, ed., *Character Portraits*, p. 192.

2. T. Jefferson to W. Jones, Jan. 2, 1814, Andrew Lipscomb and Albert E. Bergh, eds., *The Writings of Thomas Jefferson*, XIV (Washington: Jefferson Memorial Association, 1903), p. 48.

3. J. Adams to B. Rush, Apr. 15, 1808 in Page Smith, *John Adams*, II (Garden City, N.Y.: Doubleday, 1962), p. 1084; GW to B. Fairfax, Jan. 20, 1799, *Writings*, XXXVII, 94–95.

4. T. Jefferson to W. Jones, Jan. 2, 1814, *Jefferson Writings*, XIV, 50.

Selected Bibliography

What follows is an annotated list of some of those works which I found most useful in the writing of this biography; it should be considered as a supplement to the citations for, although some items are duplicated, generally I only discuss books and articles which I did not find it necessary to cite. No attempt has been made to make this an all-inclusive listing of works pertaining to Washington and his times; that kind of bibliography can be found in Freeman's volumes VI and VII and at the end of each of Flexner's four volumes. Additional help, for items of general interest, is in the bibliographies of each of the relevant volumes in the New American Nation Series, edited by Richard B. Morris and Henry Steele Commager (New York: Harper and Row, 1954–   ).

The most useful modern biographies of Washington are the Freeman and Flexner works mentioned in the preface. Older works that still retain some value are: John Marshall, *George Washington,* 5 vols. (1804–1807, rpt. Fredericksburg, Va.: Citizen's Guild of Washington's Boyhood Home, 1926); Washington Irving, *George Washington,* 5 vols. (New York: G. P. Putnam, 1855–62); Henry Cabot Lodge, *George Washington,* 2 vols. (Boston: Houghton, Mifflin, 1889); Paul Leicester Ford, *The True George Washington* (Philadelphia: Lippincott, 1896); Rupert Hughes, *George Washington,* 3 vols. (New York: Morrow, 1926–30); John C. Fitzpatrick, *George Washington Himself* (Indianapolis: Bobbs-Merrill, 1933) and Nathaniel Wright Stephenson and Waldo H. Dunn, *George Washington,* 2 vols. (New York: Oxford Univ. Press, 1940).

Representative of the iconoclastic, debunking school of the early 20th century is W. E. Woodward's *George Washington: the Image and the Man* (New York: Boni and Liveright, 1926); it is useful chiefly for its unconscious revelation of how uncritical the public attitude toward Washington was thought to be. One of the chief sources of that uncritical attitude (and a good bit of Washington mythology) is Mason Locke Weems's *The Life of Washington,* edited by Marcus Cunliffe (Cambridge, Mass.: Harvard Univ. Press, 1962), a reprint of the 1809 ninth edition with an excellent introduction by Mr. Cunliffe; Weems was the apparent originator of the cherry-tree episode, a good example of the inventiveness with which he embellished his narrative. Cunliffe has also written a brief study, *George Washington: Man and Monument* (1958, rpt. New York: New American Library, n.d.), filled with interesting interpretations. Another English scholar of American history, Esmond Wright, has given us an excellent short life in his *Washington and the American Revolution* (New York: Collier, 1962). Samuel Eliot Morison's essay "Young Man Washington," in *By Land and By Sea: Essays and Addresses by Samuel Eliot Morison* (New York: Knopf, 1953) has acute and penetrating observations on Washington's character; it is conveniently reprinted in *George Washington: A Profile*, edited by James Morton Smith (New York: Hill and Wang, 1969), a collection of worthwhile essays and excerpts delineating different aspects of Washington. Bernhard Knollenberg was the most critical modern student of Washington's career; his two books are solidly based and thought-provoking: *George Washington: the Virginia Period, 1732–1775* (Durham, N.C.: Duke Univ. Press, 1964) and *Washington and the Revolution, A Reappraisal: Gates, Conway and the Continental Congress* (1940, rpt. New York: Archon, 1968).

Washington's correspondence and other writings are easily available in the inclusive edition of his *Writings*, edited by John C. Fitzpatrick, 37 vols. (Washington: GPO, 1931–38). The complete deposit of his papers at the Library of Congress has been microfilmed and is available at selected libraries throughout the country. Fitzpatrick also edited *The Diaries of George Washington*, 4 vols. (Boston: Houghton, Mifflin, 1925). Jared Sparks's edition of Washington's writings (Boston: Russell et al., 1834) has been justly condemned for its editor's corrections of Washington's grammar and unmentioned deletions, but it does include some material now lost and is useful also for Sparks's informed comments and appendixes, e.g., a collection of correspondence relevant to the Conway Cabal in Vol. V. Stanislaus Murray Hamilton edited a collection of *Letters to Washington*, 5 vols. (Boston: Houghton, Mifflin, 1898–1902). William S. Baker edited two useful collections of impressions of Washington, *Character Portraits of Washington* (Philadelphia: Lindsay, 1887) and *Early Sketches of George Washington* (Philadelphia: Lippincott, 1894), which include some contemporary material. Gilbert Chinard did the same thing, but from a special point of view: *George Washington as the French Knew Him* (Princeton: Princeton Univ. Press, 1940). Washington's step-grandson wrote down his reminiscences of the general, thereby adding only more details to the Washington myth: George Washington Parke Custis, *Recollections and Private Memoirs of Washington*, notes by Benson J. Lossing (New York: Derby & Jackson, 1860).

Some works dealing with Virginia in Washington's time and his life at Mount Vernon are: Charles W. Stetson, *Washington and His Neighbors* (Richmond: Garrett and Massie, 1956); Moncure Daniel Conway, *Barons of the Potomack and Rappahannock* (New York: The Grolier Club, 1892); Charles Moore, *The Family Life of George Washington* (Boston: Houghton, Mifflin, 1926); Benson J. Lossing, *Mount Vernon and Its Associations, Historical, Biographical and Pictorial* (New York: W. A. Townsend, 1859); Paul Wilstach, *Mount Vernon: Washington's Home and the Nation's Shrine* (Garden City, N.Y.: Doubleday, 1925). Paul Leland Haworth, *George Washington, Country Gentleman* (Indianapolis: Bobbs, Merrill, 1925) is very good on Washington's farming practices. Charles O. Paullin discusses what

Washington's birthplace may have been like in "The Birthplace of George Washington," *William and Mary College Quarterly Historical Magazine*, 2 s., XIV (1934), 1–8. Stephen Decatur, Jr., gives interesting glimpses of Washington's personal life-style in *Private Affairs of George Washington: From the Records and Accounts of Tobias Lear, Esquire, His Secretary* (Boston: Houghton, Mifflin, 1933).

Some studies of Washington's early career and his life-long interest in the West are: John P. Cowan, "George Washington at Fort Necessity," *Western Pennsylvania Historical Magazine*, 37 (1954–55), 153–77; Frederick Tilberg, "Washington's Stockade at Fort Necessity," *Pennsylvania History*, XX (1953), 240–57; Hugh Cleland, ed., *George Washington in the Ohio Valley* (Pittsburgh: Univ. of Pittsburgh Press, 1955); Charles H. Ambler, *George Washington and the West* (Chapel Hill: Univ. of North Carolina Press, 1936); Ray Bird Cook, *Washington's Western Lands* (Strasburg, Va.: Shenandoah Publishing House, 1930). William J. Showalter describes the terrain and gives excellent maps in "The Travels of George Washington," *National Geographic Magazine*, LXI (1932), 1–63.

An old, but still useful, study is Thomas G. Frothingham's *Washington, Commander in Chief* (Boston: Houghton, Mifflin, 1930); Oliver L. Spaulding, Jr., describes Washington's military reading in "The Military Studies of George Washington," *American Historical Review*, XXIX (1923–24), 675–80. Emily Stone Whiteley's *Washington and his Aides-de-Camp* (New York: Macmillan, 1936), although adoring in tone, is useful for its delineation of who served and their period of service. Allen French, *The First Year of the American Revolution* (Boston: Houghton, Mifflin, 1934), has packed much detail into his narrative. Marshall Smelser, "George Washington Declines the Part of El Libertador," *William and Mary Quarterly*, 3 s., XI (1954), 42–51, describes a little-known incident during Washington's retirement when he refused to take part in a proposed Anglo-American scheme to liberate Spain's American colonies.

Bibliographical Addenda

The following items were either overlooked or not yet published when the first edition was released in 1979. Although I knew of the project, I did not then realize that several volumes of Washington's *Diaries* had already appeared as part of the Papers of George Washington series, W. W. Abbot, chief editor, published by the University Press of Virginia. The *Diaries* are now complete, and the first four volumes (through April 1758) of the Colonial Series of the Papers have been published, along with *The Journal of the Proceedings of the President, 1793–1797*. As completed, this edition will furnish a more inclusive, error-free, and useful replacement for the Fitzpatrick Bicentennial edition published in the 1930s.

Garry Wills's *Cincinnatus: George Washington and the Enlightenment; Images of Power in Early America* (Garden City, N.Y.: Doubleday, 1984), a fine study of Washington's conscious use of classical imagery to enhance his political effectiveness and the reception of those images by his contemporaries, should be noted. Other studies of the symbolic uses to which the Father of his Country was put, both by his contemporaries and by succeeding generations, are: Daniel B. Boorstin, "The Mythologizing of George Washington" in his *The Americans: The National Experience* (New York: Random House, 1965); Jay Fliegelman, "George Washington and the Reconstituted Family" in his *Prodigals and Pilgrims: The American Revolution against Patriarchal Authority, 1750–1800* (New York: Cambridge University Press, 1982), as well as his "The Flawless American" in Lawrence J. Friedman, *Inventors of the Promised Land* (New York: Knopf, 1975); Margaret B. Klapthor and Howard A. G. Morrison, *George Washington: A Figure upon the Stage* (Washington: Smithsonian Institution, 1982); and Wendy C. Wick, *George Washington: An American Icon* (Charlottesville: University Press of Virginia, 1982). Of a more general nature, but with frequent references to Washington, is Michael Kammen's *A Season of Youth: The American Revolution and the Historical Imagination* (1978, rpt. New York: Oxford University Press, 1980).

Recently, the political history of the early presidency has received attention from two veteran students of the early Republic's politics, and their work should be noted here: Ralph Ketcham, *Presidents above Party: The First American Presidency, 1789-1829* (Chapel Hill: University of North Carolina Press, 1984), and Richard P. McCormick, *The Presidential Game: The Origins of American Presidential Politics* (New York: Oxford University Press, 1982). Both contribute substantially to our understanding of the ideological and political atmosphere in which our first president worked. Unfortunately, the same cannot be said for John R. Alden's *George Washington: A Biography*, Southern Biography Series (Baton Rouge: Louisiana State University Press, 1984), which does not add anything of consequence to our knowledge of Washington and his times.

Index